D0863146

About the Author

Tom Scott has been a litigant in more than two dozen cases involving traffic, small claims, criminal, bankruptcy, divorce, jurisdictional, and other legal matters. He is the world's leading expert on the U.S. judicial system. In court he has defeated individuals who are supposed to uphold the law—police, lawyers, and judges. He has an amazing sixteen and four win/loss record and has won his last nine battles. The remaining matters are "ties," are ongoing, or have another status. Although sometimes costly and mentally draining, his personal experience in various courts in three states over more than two decades has provided him with the best means for helping others avoid the pitfalls within the treacherous U.S. judiciary. This has been accomplished with his first book, *Stack the Legal Odds in Your Favor*. He is also coauthoring *Stack the Health Odds in Your Favor*, his third and final book. Tom focuses his life around two things: his duty and his passion. His duty is to inform people about and protect them from the *wildly* corrupt American legal system. His passion is health and fitness.

Important Notice

Although the intended purpose of this book is to aid the American public in their understanding of the U.S. legal system by informing them about it, by no means should this book be construed as a substitute for the advice or recommendations of the reader's personal attorney. The information provided herein is not legal advice or advice of any kind, and no attorney-client or confidential relationship is or should be formed by any application thereof. The author and publisher expressly disclaim all responsibility for any detrimental or adverse effects resulting from the use or application of any explanations, ideas, or information contained in this book.

First Edition	APRIL 2022
Editor	RANDY SCHNEIDER
Cover Design	TOM SCOTT
Book Design	TOM SCOTT
Publisher	 Smart Play Publishing

Tom Scott

Our American Injustice System

A Toxic Waste Dump Also Known as the World's Largest Crime Syndicate

www.oais.us

ISBN 978-0-9965929-7-0

Dedication

This book is dedicated to individuals who have been victimized by the U.S. judicial system. In particular, it is dedicated to people who have been unjustly imprisoned and, in some cases, those who have been executed or have died in U.S. jails or prisons while serving time for crimes they did not commit. But it is also dedicated to other victims—everyone who has suffered injustices and deleterious effects at the hands of police, lawyers, judges, and other officials or entities associated with the system.

One can only speculate, but this all-inclusive group must currently number well over one million. Merely listing the subset of those who have been wrongly imprisoned would be prohibitive since it is estimated that there are literally more than a hundred thousand such persons to date. Additionally, the list is a dynamic one that is growing all the time, and every one of these people—past, present, and future—should not be forgotten. While not named explicitly on this page, I sympathize with these men, women, and children.

I have personally heard about many legal calamities from family, friends, and others. The injustices they have suffered and the injustices suffered by people like them have guided me in the selection and presentation of material. I dedicate this book to all the foregoing individuals. Their tragedies have helped shape it and consequently may conceivably help others avoid becoming future victims of our country's defective legal system.

Acknowledgments

I extend my sincerest thanks and best wishes to the following individuals whose contributions were invaluable to the success of this project. Certainly, it would not have been possible without their contributions.

Randy Schneider, editor, for his hawk-eye attention to detail, his valuable input during the entire final phase of this project, and his ultra-dry sense of humor along the way

Florence Chase, my high school English teacher, who strengthened my grasp of the English language and honed my writing skill

My mother, Norma, who instilled in me the moral values I have today, the drive to never quit, and the determination to settle for nothing less than justice

Table of Contents

Foreword vi

Preface xi

Introduction...xiii

Chapter 1: The U.S. Legal System Is the World's
Largest Crime Syndicate 1

Chapter 2: How Did We Get Here?..........................7

Chapter 3: Uselessness of Oversight Boards 11

Chapter 4: The Only Legal Ways to Defeat the
Criminals... 21

Chapter 5: Luis Sanchez's Experience with the
Syndicate... 31

Chapter 6: My Experience with the Syndicate 53

Chapter 7: How to Clean and Disinfect the Toxic
Waste Dump 97

Chapter 8: Don't Just Stand There; Do Something! 109

Chapter 9: Why Should I Care?............................115

Chapter 10: Final Thoughts.................................121

Appendix 129

References 133

Foreword

Prior to serving as executive director of the Posner Center of Justice for Pro Se's, I was a teacher and high school and college basketball coach in Indiana. Beginning in 1981 I was subjected to numerous false arrests and brutalities at the hands of rogue police in Indiana. Every time I was falsely charged, I was found not guilty or the charges were dismissed. In several of the criminal cases, I represented myself—also known as *pro se*—that is, I had no lawyer. I did this because I began to realize that my lawyers did not have my best interests at heart. A lot was going on behind the scenes between my lawyers and my adversaries, so I decided to represent myself. In doing so, I had every criminal case against me dismissed.

In March 2016 I represented myself in a five-day federal court trial against my former public school corporation employer, which was represented by several law firms. I was able to convince the jury that the school corporation violated my due process rights when it terminated my employment. The jury returned a verdict in my favor and awarded me damages of over $200,000.

Judge Richard A. Posner, a highly distinguished judge who served on the United States Court of Appeals for the Seventh Circuit in Chicago for more than thirty-five years, retired from the bench after becoming disenchanted with his judicial colleagues who were disfavoring and abusing *pro se* litigants. He formed the Posner Center of Justice for Pro Se's, a national enterprise based in Chicago, Illinois, and after hearing about how I successfully represented myself in the federal trial, asked me to join him at the Posner Center and appointed me executive director.

During my work at the Posner Center and my own personal experiences battling corruption within the U.S. legal system, I gathered a wealth of information about how rogue police abuse people's rights. I also obtained similar information about how the courts go out of their way to deprive people of their rights to fairness and justice by protecting corporations and government agencies and its agents against people's claims of wrongdoing.

While I was monitoring the happenings around the country with people's cases, I ran across Tom Scott's litigation ordeals and noticed how he was aggressively dealing with the corrupt activities by lawyers and judges against him. I also noticed a book that Tom and attorney Sara Naheedy co-wrote, *Stack the Legal Odds in Your Favor*, and decided to read it. I was quite impressed with Tom and Sara's no-nonsense approach with regard to pointing out a great deal of useful information that litigants, and particularly people who represent themselves, need to know. They need to understand what to expect and how to deal with not only complex litigation matters that are sure to arise, but also what to expect from unsavory lawyers and judges. I was so impressed with their book that I wrote an Amazon review.

Tom and I began corresponding on social media and established a friendship. I started paying more attention to how Tom was handling his legal issues and was extremely impressed to see how he was standing up to the many despicable things that were thrown his way by opposing lawyers and judges. I could see that he was a litigant who wouldn't allow himself to be intimidated by the infected, devious workings of the judiciary. He reminds me of myself in many different ways in terms of how he vehemently opposes judicial corruption and isn't afraid to call out malevolent members of the judicial system.

Sadly, everyday people don't pay much attention to what is going on in the legal world *before* it affects them. I must confess; I did much the same as a young adult until that dreadful day in September 1981 when I was with my mother at the First National Bank in Valparaiso, Indiana, and was attacked, brutalized, and falsely arrested by Valparaiso police who acted more like thugs than law enforcement officers. Afterward, I had to defend myself from their bogus charges, which I indeed did, and for which I paid a heavy price since I was thereafter persecuted by rogue police and corrupt prosecutors and judges because I stood up to injustice.

Because of their retaliation, I was falsely charged with bogus criminal charges ten times, each of which I was cleared either by a not guilty verdict, by the charges being dismissed, or by a pardon from the governor on one occasion. I am a living example of the importance of paying attention to how the system truly operates. Most people think it won't happen to them, but as Tom Scott cautions, many of those same people will learn otherwise just as I did and just as Tom did. I can certainly attest to the fact that the judiciary is a corrupt enterprise or, as Tom Scott accurately describes, a crime syndicate.

At first glance, the cover image and title may look or sound extreme or exaggerated to the novice, but the evidence in this book will reveal that both are quite appropriate. As the author of a similar book in which I wrote about the injustices regarding how corruptly the government and the judiciary operate, I can relate to what Tom has been going through with the appalling actions of the lawyers and judges with whom he has had to interact during his legal ordeals.

You, the reader, will be getting real news from this book as told in a frank manner and without consideration for "political correctness." This book is great for what it is—sounding the alarm—but *Stack the Legal Odds in Your Favor* is the guide that everyone needs because it is the one that offers protection. The picture that Tom paints of the inner workings of the system is not a pretty one, but it is a true picture that all people should heed. The fiasco he has been going through, which he recounts in these pages, is a picture of what many others will similarly be forced to see at some point in their lives due to the rampant corruption in our system.

You will read about how a seemingly simple civil case in Massachusetts gave birth to a bankruptcy in California. Both were rife with corruption. In the latter case, corrupt activities included those of a judge, who refused to follow precedent, and those of a government lawyer, who concealed documents that were supposed to be provided during discovery. All this was done in order to issue a fraudulent judgment against Tom. When you read about what the system did to him, you will realize just how corrupt judges and lawyers can be and why it is important to pay attention to his warning.

People may possibly form an opinion that some of the information in this book may be overblown, as most people don't want to believe that the courts can be so wildly corrupt, but I can attest based upon my own personal experiences in the American judiciary that they are. I easily understand what Tom has faced and so eloquently wrote about in *Our American Injustice System: A Toxic Waste Dump Also Known as the World's Largest Crime Syndicate*. We should be especially thankful to Tom for writing this very enlightening book. I applaud him for his courage to stand up to the crime syndicate also known as the U.S. judiciary and for sharing his story with us through this great book.

— Brian Vukadinovich
Former Executive Director of the Posner Center of Justice for Pro Se's and Author of *Motion for Justice: I Rest My Case*

Preface

The fall from the Garden was quite drastic. The chasm that exists between then and now is enormous. Our American injustice system has also fallen from its origins just as drastically. The train wreck with which we are left today in no way resembles what the Framers envisioned or created.

There are several reasons for this, but the bottom line is that the decay has gotten worse over the past several decades—accelerating the whole time as it still is today. Individuals who should be removed from their governmental positions, if not thrown in prison, continue to disregard facts, evidence, rules, law, and the U.S. Constitution in the process of steering legal matters in the direction they want them to go. They generally do this without repercussion.

With limited exceptions, the mainstream media ignores misconduct that originates from within the system. Only smaller *real* news outlets report on what is really transpiring within it. The advent of the internet and being able to upload self-made videos to it has allowed these smaller media channels to flourish. If not for them, people who rely on audiovisual-style news would have no idea what actually transpires behind the great wizard's curtain.

My personal experiences were not the only genesis of this book. I originally intended to write two crucial books for the nation—*Stack the Legal Odds in Your Favor* and *Stack the Health Odds in Your Favor*—and then let go of the reins.

However, certain events have necessitated this work. I have been victimized too many times by corrupt personnel within the system. If it has negatively impacted me, it has done so to countless others. The driving force behind this book is the need to convince the populace that the danger is real and paramount: the system has decayed to the point that it would no longer be recognizable to the Framers if they were alive. If you think you are immune from attack because you follow the law, think again. You must take an active role—even simply by spreading the word—to stem the tide.

Introduction

Decades ago, someone would have to go through ten judges to get one bad one. Today, someone has to go through ten judges to get one *good* one. Sadly, these figures may be conservative. I've personally been before at least seventy judges in multiple states in both the state and federal judicial systems. I can count on one hand the times that they have followed the law and done their job properly. Nearly all of them are corrupt. Most are criminals. Many belong in prison.

The preceding is one reason why I wrote this book. I didn't write it because our system is a utopia chock-full of justice or because I like to write. On the contrary, I hate to write and wrote it because the system is a rotten, fetid, corrupt cesspool—or as embodied in the subtitle—a toxic waste dump also known as the world's largest crime syndicate. Therefore, the U.S. legal system will accurately be called "injustice system," "toxic waste dump," or "syndicate" throughout the remainder of this publication.

As I did with the title of this book by employing unconventional and seemingly satirical terminology, readers may notice that in its content I use the terms Federal Bureau of Iniquity, Department of Injustice, glorified unelected lawyers in black gowns, and more. I did not do this to be funny. There is absolutely no humor in anything reported in this book. The reason for this is a direct result of my schooling and background as a recovering software engineer. My analyses are always thorough, reliable, and precise. Because of the precision in my work, I call a spade a spade and therefore call the preceding institutions exactly what they really are.

This publication is not intended to be a protective guide like *Stack the Legal Odds in Your Favor*. It is intended to be another reliable smaller news source. It is a recounting or an exposé of true events related to the author's and another person's legal experiences—all supported by irrefutable facts and evidence. This work should be viewed as a lengthy news article or a reporter's marathon dialogue at the scene of an unfolding catastrophic event.

People who have committed wrongdoing and crimes will be named in this book. Unlike protection associated with any form of immunity— qualified, judicial, absolute, or otherwise—nobody will evade culpability. Government lawyers, such as Kristin Tavia Mihelic, will be named. Her misconduct will be revealed. Her crimes will be exposed.

Judge Louise DeCarl Adler will similarly be thrust into the spotlight. Her misconduct and crimes will also not escape exposure. The list of miscreants is lengthy and is constantly growing, but everyone within my purview who is responsible for their iniquitous or criminal acts will be held accountable in this true report.

Most people who have not (yet) experienced our illustrious injustice system may think the events described herein would be part of the script for a Hollywood fantasy movie—or more appropriately, a Hollywood horror flick. This is not so. Everything put forth will be supported by rock-solid evidence.

The intent of this eye-opener is to prove to readers that any outrageous system-related stories they may have heard from friends, family members, or colleagues are likely true.

It is also intended to be the proverbial whack on the side of the head that some individuals need to make them understand that being struck with the syndicate is *not* an "other person's disease." Ordinary people in Amerika must wake up to the fact that chances are high they will someday encounter the toxic waste dump also known as the world's largest crime syndicate. The information in this book is a clarion call; however, time is running out. Read onward, but fasten your seatbelts first. It's going to be one heck of a bumpy ride.....

Chapter 1: The U.S. Legal System Is the World's Largest Crime Syndicate

You can go a long way with a smile. You can go a lot farther with a smile and a gun. — **Often attributed to Al Capone**

A crime syndicate by definition[1] is:

1. a group of people or businesses that work together

2. a group of people who are involved in organized crime

3. an association of organized criminals

It has always bothered me when an uninformed person says that the injustice system is like the Mafia. It is very *unlike* the Mafia, and comparison with it is quite insulting.....to the Mafia. You see, the Mafia actually has a set of rules that it follows, and it deserves at least some credit as a result. When its members don't follow those rules, they get "whacked."

The real syndicate differs greatly. When its members break the rules, it almost always protects those responsible or even promotes them. Furthermore, if you don't disturb the Mafia, you typically will not have any problems with it. The same cannot be said for the syndicate.

The injustice system meets the first part of the definition, which involves a group of people who work together. It is unlikely anyone would disagree that that part of the definition does not apply. Regarding the rest of the definition, the keywords are "organized" and "crime" or "criminals." Despite there often being disorder in the courts, the syndicate still operates in an organized fashion. For example, people accused of a crime are arrested, appear for an arraignment, go through a trial or agree to a plea deal, and get acquitted or convicted.

Of course, this is an oversimplification, but it is provided just to prove the point.

The fact that the syndicate is regularly involved in crime is what doubters may have difficulty accepting. For anyone who feels the second two parts of the definition do not apply because of any preconceived notions, come back to this page and read the definition again after completing this book.

Now, regarding our syndicate being the largest in the world, that is also easy to illustrate. Consider the number of law enforcement officers in the United States. There are approximately 1,000,000 of them.[2] Add to this the number of judges (48,930) and prosecutors (9,488), and you get a total of 1,058,418.[3] [4] Of course, there are many thousands of support staff not included in this figure.

Only two other countries, China and India, have more police officers than the United States— about 60 percent more.[5] However, each of these countries has about 1.4 billion people, which is 325 percent more than here in the United States, so they have substantially less police per capita. China is said to have around 200,000 judges, but India has only about 20,500.[6] [7] In either case, the total per capita numbers are still smaller than here in Amerika. Neglecting prosecutors, whose numbers are conjectured to be insignificant relative to those of police and judges, this makes their judicial systems significantly smaller in terms of personnel, with China being about 2.5 times smaller and India being about 2.75 times smaller.

In terms of cost associated with salaries and infrastructure alone, the federal judiciary consumes $7.8 billion in tax dollars annually.[8] Add to this the fact that the United States spends nearly $300 billion each year to police communities and incarcerate over 2 million people. The societal costs of incarceration—lost earnings, adverse health effects, and the damage to the families of the incarcerated—are estimated at up to three times the direct costs, bringing the total burden of our criminal injustice system to $1.2 trillion.[9] Considering all costs associated with the entire syndicate and not just the criminal injustice system, the figure probably exceeds $2 trillion every year.

Looking at other nations, only China has an annual budget big enough to allow it to challenge the cost of the U.S. injustice system.[10] The yearly budget for China's legal system is approximately $220 billion.[11] Since the cost of running the syndicate here is far more than 1.36 times greater than there (using the lower $300 billion figure above, which just includes policing and incarcerating), it is clear that the money spent on the syndicate in this country is more than any other. Although China incarcerates about 1.7 million people, the second highest next to Amerika, it falls short both in terms of judicial system personnel and annual monetary expenditure.

Comparing the syndicate with the more "traditional" organized crime rings yields the same result. The South American drug cartels earn what one source considers a high-end estimate of $39 billion each year.[12] 'Ndrangheta, the Calabrian mafia, is thought to have made about $59 billion in 2013 according to another source, but a third source

4

says that the combined revenue of the entire Italian organized crime network is highly overestimated, with the annual total actually being closer to $14 billion.[13] [14] In any event, the largest preceding figure still pales in comparison.

The four main Italian mafia groups have an estimated membership of 25,000, with 250,000 affiliates worldwide.[15] One would need to combine those two numbers with the number of members of several of the largest drug cartels and gangs to come close to or eclipse syndicate personnel numbers.[16] So no matter how you slice it—legal systems in other countries, gangs, cartels, or "traditional" organized crime—the U.S. legal system is the world's largest crime syndicate in terms of both people and dollars.

Lastly, regarding the American injustice system being a toxic waste dump, the term is meant to be symbolic or dysphemistic. However, it has literally been toxic to countless people. It has even caused death in many instances—more than 15,269 in terms of executions since 1608.[17] Forgetting for the moment those who have been wrongly convicted and executed, some have died due to suicide because of the mental trauma they have suffered at the hands of corrupt judges.[18] [19] Once again, indirect impacts to individuals and families cannot be underestimated. All told, innumerable people have been negatively impacted by misconduct and crime committed by rotten people within the syndicate.

Chapter 2: How Did We Get Here?

And you may ask yourself, "Well, how did I get here?" — **David Byrne, "Once in a Lifetime"**

Answering the question of this chapter's title is slightly complicated. As a first step towards doing so, let us examine one of our traits as a species. It is human nature to gravitate towards things that match one's character and abilities. For instance, someone who can throw something with high speed or accuracy might attempt a career as a major league baseball pitcher or a quarterback in the NFL. For those who have the innate drive to solve problems, scientific and engineering professions beckon to them. Homosexual individuals might have the penchant to pursue performing arts. Lastly, bullies and criminals gravitate towards careers in the crime syndicate.

It is natural for people to tend towards things that match their persona. Painting with a broad brush is not a wise thing to do since each profession and the corresponding individual pursuing it have underlying idiosyncrasies, but the illustration was provided in order to make a point. None of the foregoing correlations are true across the board, but the proclivity is there. Since societal values have seemingly dropped over time, the pool of members available to join the syndicate is therefore larger. Note that I am not saying the syndicate is composed entirely of criminals. That would be almost impossible. What I *am* saying is that if you are looking for dirty rotten scoundrels, the injustice system is the best place to find them.

The second factor in providing the answer is the ability of our form of government to provide checks and balances—or lately, lack thereof. Checks and balances should work at least sometimes when the masses become involved. Since the syndicate basically operates in a vacuum, keeping the masses outside the realm of influence is now par for the course. Also, the judiciary is the only branch of the three whereby judges are not always elected. In places where this holds true, they essentially can't be removed from the bench. More about this topic will be explained in the next chapter.

A third factor to consider is the "frog in the pot" theory. While it has been proved to be urban legend, the concept still is relevant to human beings. Anecdotally, the principle tries to show that slow change over time can be detrimental, even lethal, to a living being—all while the victim unknowingly accepts its fate. If a frog is placed into a pot of cool water and the heat is slowly increased, the frog will not notice the difference and remain in the water— and cook. If a frog is placed into hot water, however, it will feel the large increase in temperature and immediately jump out.

Even though in reality the frog evacuates the hot water in either instance, the premise for people is still correct. People will not object to changes that negatively but slowly impact them over time. They are less apt to complain when oppression upon them worsens incrementally. The injustice system didn't become the toxic waste dump that it is overnight. Its decay began well over 100 years ago and continues today. Because of this slow and long process, people have been willing to give up their liberties, live under tyranny, and accept governmental corruption.

The last factor for providing the answer to the chapter title's question is government itself. As Churchill said, "Democracy is the worst form of government except for all those other forms that have been tried from time to time."[1] The Framers gave it their best shot to improve upon government ideology, and they did remarkably well. Perhaps the *only* mistake they made was creating a judiciary whereby many judges are appointed instead of elected—that these judges are not at all beholden to the electorate.

However, Jefferson, who *hated* big, unrestrained government, realized this: "When the legislative or executive functionaries act unconstitutionally, they are responsible to the people in their elective capacity. The exemption of the judges from that is quite dangerous enough. I know no safe depository of the ultimate powers of the society, but the people themselves."[2]

Chapter 3: Uselessness of Oversight Boards

The production of too many useful things results in too many useless people. — **Karl Marx**

Authority is *not* a problem. Authority without accountability *is* a problem. Nobody should be above the law, but here in Amerika, sadly, members of the syndicate are almost always above the law and held unaccountable. Only a few select members are ever attacked for their wrongdoing.

In a perfect world, every institution would work as it should, and any wrongdoing would be immediately and appropriately corrected. This would also be true for the injustice system. For those of us who have been victimized by it, we know this simply isn't true.

Certain oversight boards for lawyers and judges are *supposed* to address misconduct whenever it occurs and punish the offenders. The names of these boards vary nationwide. The entity tasked with overseeing judges is called the Commission on Judicial Conduct in some states. In others it is called the Commission on Judicial Performance. Additional nomenclature is found across the country.

In most instances, there are about five to twenty or so members on these boards. Typically, the overwhelming majority are lawyers and judges. Lay people usually occupy some position within these groups, but by and large, lawyers and judges are the ones calling the shots. Although many of these boards have such lay people as members, the proportions are backwards. Rather than being mostly lay people, they are mostly lawyers and judges.[1] This makes them inadequate control mechanisms.

There are similar oversight boards for lawyers. Names also vary by state. Board of Bar

Overseers is the title given in one state. Office of Chief Disciplinary Counsel is the title given in another. The name is not important. The fact that these boards are a joke *is* important. This is one thing that absolutely must change and will be discussed more in chapter seven.

The naïve think that these oversight boards within the syndicate will come to their rescue and right any wrongs. I held this misconception myself once a long time ago. After filing at least six or seven complaints like I have without any resulting remedial action being taken against the offenders, one realizes they are a pipe dream. On paper, having watchdog organizations is an excellent idea; in reality, they are just another "black hole" that swallows up your tax dollars.

The injustice system cannot police itself, nor can any entity that has a conflict of interest. Lawyers and judges are rarely reprimanded, much less removed. In order for these boards to step in and take any remedial action whatsoever, syndicate members must do something extremely egregious— almost kill someone, for example, and I'm not exaggerating. Not only that, but they have to piss off the wrong people. If both these conditions are not met, the guilty walk free.

Specifically regarding federal judges, the evidence indisputably reveals that they are untouchable and remain on the bench despite wrongdoing or corruption. The record clearly shows that almost all complaints against them are dismissed outright. In 2015 there were 1,214 complaints filed against federal judges, and not a single one of them resulted in remedial action.[2] In fact, only 12 out of 7,773 complaints filed from 2015 through 2020—almost one out of a thousand, or about a mere 0.1 percent—resulted in any form of disciplinary action. This is completely ridiculous.

Statistics for judicial misconduct at the state level—when they can be found—are equally mind-boggling. The syndicate tries its best to conceal the data; however, some were found for the state of New York, albeit somewhat old. The numbers discovered for that state are about ten times better than at the federal level, but 1 percent is still quite abysmal. Out of the 1,418 complaints filed in 1976, only thirteen resulted in any meaningful action—that being suspension, removal, or resignation. Although I cannot prove it, I would venture to say that the reprimand rate has dropped since then.

Also with respect to judges, in only approximately eleven states is a judge always removed from the bench when he or she is convicted of certain types of crimes—not all crimes, just certain ones.3 If this is not jaw-dropping to you, then I don't know what the hell is. Our injustice system is *so bad* that being convicted of a crime is still not enough to remove the criminal in the black gown in the majority of states!

AN EXAMPLE OF USELESSNESS

One particular high-profile example of the uselessness of oversight boards concerns a federal judge in Texas, Edith Jones of the Fifth Circus Court of Appeals. In 2006 the *Texas Observer* dubbed her one of the "worst judges in Texas," in part because of her decision to uphold the death sentence for a man whose lawyer slept through the entire trial. She has been especially hostile to sexual harassment claims, once dismissing such lawsuits in a Federalist Society speech as "petty interoffice disputes." In one instance, a woman provided graphic testimony about the severe sexual harassment and abuse she had suffered at work, saying that a male co-worker had pinched her buttocks with a pair of pliers and another had pinched her breast. Jones replied to the latter charge, "Well, he apologized."

At least one known complaint has been filed against her, which was handled by Merrick B. Garland, current U.S. Attorney General but judge at the time. The 2013 complaint stemmed from a speech Jones gave at the University of Pennsylvania Law School. According to people who were at the event and the complaint they filed afterward, Jones made several inflammatory comments, including the suggestion that black and Hispanic people are "predisposed to crime" and "prone" to violence. She allegedly said it was a "disservice to the mentally retarded to exempt them from the death penalty," and that the evidence of their planning and involvement in crimes proves that such individuals are not in fact disabled.

Several of the attendees, including some assistant federal defenders, the National Bar Association, the Texas Civil Rights Project, the League of United Latin American Citizens (LULAC), and other groups determined that Jones's audacious, racist, and prejudicial comments—including those referring to cases pending on her docket—warranted censure and remedial action against her. Thus, they filed an ethics complaint.

In order to give the façade of impartiality, the Fifth Circus chief judge referred the case to Supreme Court Chief Justice John Roberts Jr., who then handed it to Garland, who appointed a special committee of three D.C. Circus judges to handle the complaint: Garland and two other judges. The committee, in turn, recruited Jeffrey Bellin, a professor at William & Mary Law School, to conduct the factual investigation.

Since most complaints get filed under "G" upon entry into the system, it is unusual that this one made it this far. But the complaint against Jones garnered considerable media attention, partly because some judicial watchdog groups publicly pushed Garland to conduct a serious inquiry. Only when it is difficult to sweep complaints against lawyers and judges under the rug do they get this kind of attention by oversight boards.

People for the American Way, the civil liberties group founded by Norman Lear, wrote a petition asking signers to "Urge Judge Garland to make the investigation swift and thorough and to hold Edith Jones accountable for any comments that show her unable to be a fair and impartial judge." Alliance for Justice sent Garland a letter supporting the complaint. Both groups had backed Garland's nomination to the Supreme Court. In fact, Alliance for Justice praised him as "an extraordinarily accomplished and highly qualified jurist who will bring thoughtfulness, intellect, and a passionate respect for the law to the nation's highest court."

Only two people were allowed to testify before Garland's committee during the investigation of Jones: Jones herself and Marc Bookman, a

Philadelphia death penalty lawyer who attended her speech and helped file the complaint. Maurie Levin, one of the lawyers for the complainants, said the investigation was "blanketed in secrecy and bias." She noted that although Bookman was cross-examined by Jones's attorney, Jones testified in secret, without any of the complainants in the room. The fact that this happened is clearly a red flag, if not an alarm bell, that remediating the complaint correctly had the same chance as a snowball surviving more than one year in hell.

An investigative report was issued by Garland's panel. According to it, Jones denied the worst of the charges but admitted that she made some of the comments, including the one whereby she said she was skeptical of claims of intellectual disability among death penalty defendants. But Levin said that the panel refused to disclose the documents she filed in her defense or a transcript of her testimony.

Garland and the other judges on the special committee ultimately "found" that Jones had not violated the judicial code of ethics, in large part because her speech had not been recorded and the evidence was not sufficient. How convenient this is. They recommended that the judicial council of the D.C. Circus, which had final say in the matter, dismiss the complaint. Of course, this is exactly what it did.

"The judicial panel that investigated the complaint—presided over by Judge Garland—twisted itself into a pretzel to find that Judge Jones would face no consequences, and dismissed the complaint," said Levin. "It is difficult to imagine that action instilled confidence in Judge Jones's impartiality in the African American and Hispanic communities." She said the process raises the question of whether Garland and his fellow judges were "more interested in protecting [their] brethren than rooting out bias in the administration of justice." The record is fairly clear. The former is true, while the latter is false.

Civil rights groups appealed the decision, writing, "At its core, the decision of the [judges] serves to undermine any faith the public may have in the fairness and impartiality of the judiciary, the federal judicial discipline system or a system free of race bias." Luis Roberto Vera, Jr., LULAC's national general counsel, said in a press release, "Just as concerning as these instances of bias, the one-sidedness and secrecy surrounding the ethics complaint process and the untoward deference to the judge's denials makes it unlikely that any claims of judicial misbehavior can be handled in a way that gives the public confidence that justice is being served."

Unsurprisingly, a different panel of federal judges upheld the earlier decision made by Garland panel's and dismissed the complaint permanently against Jones a year later. Andrew Cohen, a CBS commentator and lawyer who has written extensively about the death penalty, tweeted at the time: "Farce of the Day: How federal judges herded together to protect Fifth Circuit Judge Edith Jones, a national disgrace." Circling the wagons is a common occurrence with the syndicate.

Unfortunately, the advocacy groups that had urged Garland to reprimand Jones never expressed much outrage about the decision to dismiss the complaint. Alliance for Justice noted the dismissal of the complaint in a press release but directed most of its message at criticizing Jones instead of Garland. A People for the American Way spokeswoman said her organization had pushed for a full investigation into the allegations, "which did occur." She pointed out that another federal judge who was not involved in the case, Richard Kopf of the U.S. District Court in Nebraska, had examined the charges in a blog post and sided with Garland.

Kopf wrote that while Jones "is far too right-wing for my tastes" and her "speaking styles can be blunt," he nonetheless felt that the allegations against her were thin and threatened to chill the speech of federal judges who are encouraged to speak publicly about the law. He said Garland's panel had appropriately considered whether a controversial speech was a violation of the judicial code of ethics and that the report "makes me proud to be a federal judge." I bet it does. Garland's committee, he wrote, deserved "high praise for teaching us a lot about federal judicial ethics in the real world."[4] I think almost everyone will agree the committee does not deserve "high praise," but it certainly teaches us "a lot about federal judicial ethics in the real world."

This particular example was provided to show that the syndicate is reluctant to reprimand any offenders—despite facts, evidence, or pressure by large organizations. If an offense as blatant as Jones's results in a complaint being filed by high-powered associations but does not result in any form of discipline, then any complaint you file against a lawyer or judge has a zero chance of success .....maybe less.

As it stands now, mechanisms in place to correct misconduct are failing miserably. There are much better ways to remove the bad apples throughout the entire injustice system. These are discussed in chapter seven.

Chapter 4: The Only Legal Ways to Defeat the Criminals

With governments, you don't always get a fair word or a fair fight.
— **Clint Eastwood,** *The Outlaw Josey Wales*

It would be understandable for someone to think that the easiest way to dispose of corrupt members of the syndicate is to cap them. Actually, I'm quite surprised this does not happen more often. However, any sane person needs to understand that if a syndicate criminal is taken out, there is essentially an infinite supply of others standing ready right behind him ready to pop in and take his place. The *underlying problem* is what needs to be solved. Besides being illegal, of course, whacking these vermin would not do much good.

Until the root of the problem is addressed, however, there are several legal ways to defeat them, which is the purpose of this chapter. As mentioned in the front matter, this is not a how-to guide, but instead is a book about enlightenment. This chapter will continue that theme.

A crucial point—the most important one in this book—needs to be made about winning and losing battles in the syndicate's arena. In reality, three different outcomes are possible:

1. If the syndicate likes your adversary, *whether or not* it plays by the syndicate's rules, you will lose every case every single time if you play by those same rules.

2. If the syndicate does not like you, you will lose every case every single time if you play by its rules.

3. Regardless of who the syndicate likes, if you follow the "rules" in this chapter or employ similar guerrilla tactics, you may not win, but your odds of winning increase by orders of magnitude.

If you think as a *pro se* litigant that you can make a great argument and have all the facts, evidence, rules, law, and Constitution on your side—and you might—and that this will ensure your victory, think again. You could write a Pulitzer Prize masterpiece and run circles around the monkeys in the government entity or whatever big business is opposing you, but it could be to no avail.

Understand that in a best-case scenario when fighting as a self-represented litigant, your papers are likely going to be read and ruled upon by a staff attorney in the courthouse or occasionally by a magistrate or judge. In a worst-case scenario when battling a governmental or big-business adversary, your paperwork will be completely ignored by government personnel at the courthouse and only read by your opposition whose people will write all rulings and orders in the case that the judge will then rubber-stamp. The judge will merely make it appear to the novice as though the judge is the writer when in effect she is simply signing whatever your opposition has provided her. An example of this is given in the Conflicts of Interest subsection of chapter six.

In a scathing American Bar Association article, the most cited legal scholar of all time and perhaps the best appellate judge in the entire history of the United States, Richard Posner, said, "The basic thing is that most judges regard [people who represent themselves] as [a] kind of trash not worth the time of a federal judge."[1][2] The irony of all this is the same as the irony when Jesus Christ was executed roughly 2,000 years ago. The criminals regarded *him* as the criminal. A parallel evidently

23

occurs in the courts. The trash regard *pro se* litigants as trash. On a side note, the injustice system has only gotten worse over the last two millennia.

As reported in that same article, this great judge then went on to say: "staff lawyers review appeals from *pro se* litigants, and their recommendations are generally rubber-stamped by judges." Posner went so far as to offer to help *pro se* litigants by reviewing all of the staff attorney memos before they went to the panel of judges. He had approval from the director of the staff attorney program. "But the judges, my colleagues, all eleven of them, turned it down and refused to give me any significant role. I was very frustrated by that," Posner said.[3]

He has also publicly stated, "We have a very crappy judicial system. That's the long and short of it. And that contaminates much of government." Continuing, he said, "The theory of our judicial system is that the lawyers pick all the witnesses and make all the arguments, and the judge is just an arbitrator, basically. I find that very unsatisfactory because I don't trust the lawyers."[4] If only other judges would come to realize as he does, "that this wasn't right, what we were doing," it would be a giant step towards resolving the problem and restoring the injustice system to the shining example of *justice* that it once was.[5]

Mr. Posner's sentiments are not unfounded. They are also not unusual. Approval of the U.S. Supreme Court by Americans is only at 40 percent, which is a new low. Trust of the entire federal judiciary is also near an all-time low at 54 percent.[6]

It is the second lowest rating in almost forty years and is only one percentage point away from being tied for lowest. Such figures are not unexplainable.

"The former jurist said he retired from the bench because the justice system was far from just when it came to *pro se* litigants. He explained that judges would often copy and paste from briefs submitted by seasoned lawyers when writing their opinions, giving *pro se* litigants the impression their motions were not independently analyzed and emphasizing the power imbalance between *pro se* litigants and opposing counsel, which is an abdication of the judge's official duty as a neutral arbiter."[7]

I know that what Mr. Posner described happened in my very own case. The writings from the Department of Injustice attorney who was opposing me, Kristin Tavia Mihelic, had clearly been either copied and pasted with slight modifications so as to create all the judicial rulings and orders in my bankruptcy or Mihelic wrote two versions of everything she submitted to the court. In the latter case, one was entered into the docket in the form of a motion or an objection, and another was given directly to the judge for rubber-stamping as the "official" order/ruling on that motion or objection. In many instances, the syndicate tried to hide in plain sight the fact that Mihelic was writing the court orders. See the appendix for just one example.

Keeping the preceding in mind, you must therefore employ unorthodox methodologies if you value your property or life, as the case may be, when the syndicate is gunning for you. If it is, this brings us to my next point. Recall from the American

Revolutionary War how the fledgling nation fought the British Army. The colonists didn't march in a straight line like the British soldiers did. If they had, they would have gotten slaughtered. Instead, they hid behind rocks and trees only popping out of their hiding places to take a shot. Immediately afterward, they would fall back under cover.

Events of that time saw the birth of guerrilla warfare in this country. This style of fighting is *precisely* the same kind you must employ to survive the onslaught of the syndicate. A short primer on the subject is given in the movie *Enemy of the State*. At one point in it, Gene Hackman's character, Edward "Brill" Lyle, is talking with Will Smith's character, Robert Dean, in a diner scene just before they go after the federal agents. Brill begins the lesson with: "You know, in guerrilla warfare, you try to use your weaknesses as strengths. Well, if they're big and you're small, then you're mobile and they're slow. You're hidden and they're exposed. You only fight battles you know you can win. That's the way the Vietcong did it. You capture their weapons, and then you use them against them the next time. That way they're supplying you. You grow stronger as they grow weaker."

Some related strategies are discussed in the following sections. These are not for the faint of heart, but one thing to keep in mind while reading ahead is that almost *nobody* in the nation attempts these things. That is a huge advantage for you because syndicate criminals are not used to having someone oppose or fight them. To the contrary, they—especially judges—are used to ruling the nest and having everyone cower to them. If you have the stomach to carry out any of the following examples of guerrilla warfare, you will be three steps ahead of everyone else.

PUT SYNDICATE MEMBERS IN PRISON

This may be laughable, but in a perfect world, it would certainly do the trick. Of course, as it stands today with the injustice system, this is a bluff more than anything else, but it may work. The chance of this tactic being successful is slim to none, but I don't like to hide any available weaponry from view. I place everything for selection on the table: the knife, the revolver, the battle ax, and more—nothing is withheld—and you pick whatever you think will work best in your situation.

For instance, you could contact (or threaten to contact) the Department of Injustice, the Federal Bureau of Iniquity, the Office of "Professional" Responsibility, the Office of the Inspector General, the oversight boards mentioned in chapter three, and other similar entities and file complaints or demand an investigation. Depending upon your circumstances, you could also hire a private investigator to unearth whatever evidence you need before approaching the preceding organizations. If you are skilled at searching the internet and have enough time, you may be able to obtain much evidence yourself. If you do not, hiring a PI is a sound alternative. A qualified PI can be quite helpful. I've had good success with such investigators in the past.

HIT SYNDICATE MEMBERS IN THE WALLET

The remainder of the tactics in this chapter, including this one—hitting syndicate members in the wallet—have a more realistic shot at helping you achieve victory. I did exactly this to one judge-criminal, which I describe in the Louise DeCarl Adler subsection of chapter six. I told her that I would be attacking her character via online reviews of her rental properties and then modify the search engine optimization so that my reviews would be found first, with the end result being that she would not rent her units to anyone ever again. She was so afraid of me and didn't know how to react that she put her condominiums on the market the very next day.

Remember that sources of income are not limited to just rental properties. Many government officials have side businesses, or their spouses do. If you are backed into a corner and are forced to go for the throat, by all means, go for the throat! Anything is fair game. One government attorney fighting me in my latest case, Abram Stuart Feuerstein, is an art collector. I am already threatening to have the IRS investigate him. It all boils down to thinking of ways either to reduce or stop their flow of income or take away some or all of the income they have already accumulated.

One of the ways to do the latter is to file a lawsuit. I did exactly this when I filed a $2.2 million civil case against Judge Adler, Kristin Tavia Mihelic, and Tiffany Louise Carroll. They are all federal government employees involved in my bankruptcy and committed misconduct and crimes throughout it. More will be told about them in chapter six, but for now, understand that you *can* fight these criminals. It is not easy to win monetary judgments, particularly against federal officials, but it can be done. Conditions for winning are better when their government attorneys make mistakes, which they frequently do. Conditions will also improve if you are fortunate enough to get a judge that actually follows the rules and law. Odds of this are obviously quite low, but there is a possibility.

GIVE THE SYNDICATE NEGATIVE PR

The syndicate really hates negative press. In fact, the mainstream media only does its job with respect to reporting nefarious syndicate activity when it has been given the green light from another part of the syndicate. If you recall the "kids for cash" scandal, state court judges got bagged for committing many heinous crimes. The only reason we heard about it is that federal agents came down on them. Since this arm of the syndicate was involved against a state arm of the syndicate, the press was allowed to report the incident.

Operation Greylord is another example of one arm attacking another and also why mainstream media was permitted to report it. I have tried repeatedly to get the mainstream media involved in my saga of corruption, but no interest has been shown to put it in print because I am fighting the *entire* syndicate and have not been able to get one part of it to square off against another. Many people in my national network have gotten the same results. Although I cannot prove it unequivocally, the mainstream media is the lap dog of the syndicate.

Whatever the syndicate says is what the main media outlets do.

This all means that you will most likely be on your own to generate any negative PR. You could do this by blogging, by using social media, by starting your own news source, and many other ways. With the advent of the internet and online video channels in particular, starting your own news source is relatively easy and cheap, if not free. Many real and reliable news sources can be found on YouTube and other video streaming sites. In the last couple of decades, the most reliable have been the smaller outlets. All of the larger news "channels" on both sides of the political aisle are more concerned with ratings, revenue, and causing conflict between the two main political parties rather than delivering real news.

Lastly, one final option to generate negative PR is to write a book like this one. There are many books on the market today, but only a relatively small number of them address corruption with the injustice system. And only two known works actually provide people with ways to counter it: *Stack the Legal Odds in Your Favor* and *You Have the Right to Remain Innocent*. Once again, the technological age has streamlined things that used to be cumbersome and costly and made them fairly simple and inexpensive, book publishing being one such endeavor.

Chapter 5: Luis Sanchez's Experience with the Syndicate

The only thing more painful than learning from experience is not learning from experience. — **Anonymous**

As unbelievable as it will be to the uninformed reader, the events in this chapter and the next will seem to defy rationale—that they cannot possibly happen here in Amerika. I assure you they do happen and not infrequently either. They happen every day in every court in every state across the nation. And it is horrifying. In fact, the common denominator with respect to laws that are most frequently violated by members of the syndicate in court proceedings—as demonstrated by the examples in these two chapters—happens to be these top seven given in no particular order:

- perjury

- misprision of felony

- fraud

- conspiracy to commit fraud

- obstruction of justice

- withholding/falsifying/manipulating evidence

- falsifying judicial and public records and documents

Other than how *wildly* corrupt our injustice system is, this point is perhaps the second most important one in this book. If you've never personally experienced any of these crimes being committed in your legal matters by syndicate members, either you have not been involved with our famed syndicate (yet), or you don't know the rules and laws well enough to know that the syndicate has been violating them against you.

There is also the possibility you have only interacted with the syndicate minimal times and have been extremely fortunate that it has followed its own rules and laws. But it is a virtual guarantee that the more you are exposed to it, the more the chances will approach 100 percent that you will fall prey to it. A final remotely possible reason you may have not been a victim of any of the aforementioned crimes is that you are on the "right team" and thus are either part of or liked by the syndicate, in which case you would almost certainly not be reading this exposé in the first place.

This chapter and the next form the very heart of this book. As nauseating or disgusting you may find them, you must face the fact that this is how the syndicate truly operates—and that you or a loved one will almost certainly someday experience the misconduct described in these chapters in some form or another during time here on Earth. Central to the discussion in these two chapters is the fact that bad members of the syndicate will do whatever they can to get the outcome they want if they do not like someone who opposes them.

To introduce this chapter and the next, an analogy is helpful. Consider the 100-meter sprint in the Olympics. In the real world, spectators fill the stands, watch the competitors take their marks, hear the start gun, and watch the sprinters race towards the finish line. They clearly see who finishes first and who finishes last.

The syndicate's rendition of the race differs significantly. The race itself is the same, but the stands are empty. All spectators are forced to wait outside the stadium. The only people who see the race are the sprinters themselves and the race officials. After the finish, the officials convene and talk among themselves to determine if they like the winner. If they don't, they pick an alternate. In this analogy, it so happens that they like the sprinter who finished dead last. They declare her the new winner and even ask her how big she wants the recorded margin of victory to be, which she herself writes on the scorecard. Then they put the winner in last place by wrongly doctoring their scorecard to reflect the interchanging of the two positions.

The officials then go outside the stadium to talk with the anxiously awaiting press and spectators. They tell them about the "results" of the race and show them the "scorecard," which is the "official record" of the race. The press and spectators are led to believe the results are exactly as the officials say they are because they did not see what really transpired. They did not see the race itself. They did not see the officials manipulate the results. All they see is whatever the officials have written in the record, and all they hear is whatever they have been told.

This is precisely how the syndicate operates. Its members concoct court records so that they can make case results fit their desired narrative. Shielded from public view, the syndicate picks the winners ahead of time and then ensures that cases are driven from point "A" to point "B" by manipulating facts and evidence and violating rules of court and law. It's an eminence front; it's a put on.[1]

Jonathan Zell, a highly respected attorney from Columbus, Ohio, believes that the whole system is a fraud. According to Zell, personal biases of judges interfere with them upholding justice. Trial judges first decide what they want the results of a case to be and then—when events would not normally drive it in that direction—select whatever case law and thinly veiled reasons justify their decisions, a corrupt process that appellate courts usually cover up with more of the same. Lost in the process are the facts of the case and the true controlling law.

Zell is a current member of the Committee on Ethics and Professionalism of the Judicial Division of the American Bar Association (ABA) whereby he continually offers commonsense proposals to control corrupt judges, but the pro-judge ABA keeps rejecting those proposals. Zell is one of few attorneys in the country who has the integrity and courage to constructively criticize the syndicate and actually recommend such proposals to the ABA.

In line with Zell's beliefs, I have said for some time that the injustice system is like a jigsaw puzzle. But unlike a normal puzzle that will produce the same picture no matter who assembles it, depending upon who is assembling the injustice system puzzle and which pieces that person chooses, it can produce a different picture every single time.

The preceding discussion means that if and when you view a court record, it is quite likely that whatever you read with your own eyes *in no way reflects* what actually happened in the case. This fact will be illustrated in the balance of this chapter and the next and hopefully dispel any notions you may have that the tooth fairy really does exist.

THE GROSS INJUSTICE DIRECTED AT LUIS SANCHEZ

The following is a step-by-step accounting and analysis of what really happened in Mr. Sanchez's case as the facts actually relate to the false narrative provided in the court record. A video of the horrifying events that took place on March 19, 2018, was obtained by Mr. Sanchez and is available for viewing at www.oais.us/sanchez.php. The original was posted on YouTube and can still be found there as of this writing, but since I do not trust the syndicate any further than I can throw it and fear it may be removed, a backup has been uploaded to the previous link.

As you read the remainder of this chapter, stop periodically and put yourself in Mr. Sanchez's shoes and think about how you would have reacted. Also during those pauses, think about how many times the responsible criminals who inhabit the toxic waste dump have committed these reprehensible acts before and since then across the nation. Finally, understand that next time this could be you.

TRASH FOUND IN THE TOXIC WASTE DUMP

The waste materials named in the following subsections are some of the miscreants who have been involved with Mr. Sanchez's case. The list is not intended to be exhaustive. Many of them belong in prison. Their roles in the wrongdoing associated with the syndicate in his matter will be explained further in the next section of this chapter.

Jared Brooks Cardon

The case against Mr. Sanchez began when he was arrested by Officer Cardon. This is the same officer who was later charged with being high on fentanyl after crashing his police vehicle while on duty June 12, 2021. He was also charged with carrying a dangerous weapon under the influence of drugs, driving under the influence, possession or use of a controlled substance, and possession or use of a firearm by a restricted person. This upstanding citizen had also been previously charged with reckless endangerment for shooting at a fleeing motorist when he was with the West Valley City police and resigned before joining the Unified Police Department.[2]

Katherine Bernards-Goodman

Bernards-Goodman is the glorified unelected lawyer in a black gown who presided over at least a portion of Mr. Sanchez's case. She was appointed in 2010 to the position she held at the time of the hearing on March 19, 2018, which forms the basis for the analysis in this chapter. She was also sued in an unrelated case in 2015.[3] Apparently, she retired on September 1, 2019. It is uncertain whether her criminal involvement with Mr. Sanchez's case played a role in her retirement since she was only about 63 years of age when she announced her retirement in early 2019. Without a doubt, she should have been prosecuted and thrown in prison.

Michael F. Skolnick

Skolnick is an attorney who represents the Salt Lake Legal Defender Association and the public defenders named in the lawsuit Mr. Sanchez has been forced to bring against them and said that Sanchez's suit was "not well-grounded in fact or law." He went on to lie further: "Mr. Sanchez's complaint omits important factual context and misstates several key facts."[4] He is a typical bottom-feeding attorney who *knows* his clients committed crimes, yet will *pretend* they did not and *lie* in order to defend them anyway. Instead of simply saying, "We anticipate vigorously defending against Mr. Sanchez's claims," he had to add the lies. He is the same kind of attorney as George Vincent Manahan who is named in the next chapter.

Daniel Mcadam Torrence

Torrence is a court-appointed public "defender." He conspired with Heather J. Chesnut, Bernards-Goodman, and possibly others in order to get a fraudulent arrest warrant issued for Mr. Sanchez. Torrence is also named as a defendant in a civil lawsuit Sanchez filed.

Heather Johnson Chesnut

Chesnut is also a court-appointed public "defender." She conspired with Torrence, Bernards-Goodman, and possibly others in order to get the fraudulent arrest warrant issued for Mr. Sanchez. She is also named as a defendant in the same civil suit Sanchez filed as mentioned in the previous subsection.

Nathanael L. Swift

Swift is the prosecutor in the original criminal case against Mr. Sanchez. Remarkably, he appears to be the least corrupt of all the government personnel in this chapter. This is a bit unusual since prosecutors are often—along with the glorified lawyers in black gowns—the most corrupt of the bunch.

THE INFECTION

Corruption in the injustice system is so bad that its criminals cannot even keep their stories straight in just one official court document. The minutes from a hearing at the Third District Court in Salt Lake County Utah recorded on March 19, 2018, are shown in the appendix.

On the first page, the court minutes state that Mr. Sanchez "failed to appear" at the hearing. The video obtained of the scene of the crime(s) clearly shows him in the courtroom. Keep in mind that none of the misconduct shown in the video is reflected anywhere in the court records for the criminal case against him.[5] To the untrained eye reading just those records, it will seem that Luis Sanchez has been properly painted as Charles Manson and the syndicate as Mother Teresa.

On the second page, the court minutes state: "Case is called to advise [D]efendant he is being taken in to custody on the outstanding warrant".....that the criminals issued moments before. How could they possibly advise Mr. Sanchez on the very same day in the very same court of his "failure to appear" if he was never there? This is complete nonsense.

The minutes also reveal on page two that what the syndicate did at approximately 8:45 a.m. was illegal since clearly written on this page is a statement that the pretrial conference was to be held at "09:00 a.m." In a mere *one* court record, the syndicate managed to violate at least five state criminal laws, one federal criminal law, and two clauses of the U.S. Constitution—cruel and unusual punishment of the Eighth Amendment and due process of the Fourteenth Amendment. The relevant laws are the following:

- *76-6-504. Tampering with records — Penalty.*
  (1) Any person who, having no privilege to do so, knowingly falsifies, destroys, removes, or conceals any writing, other than the writings enumerated in Section 76-6-503.5 for which the law provides public recording or any record, public or private, with intent to deceive or injure any person or to conceal any wrongdoing is guilty of tampering with records.

- *76-8-504.6 False or misleading information.*
  (1) A person is guilty of a class B misdemeanor if the person, not under oath or affirmation, intentionally or knowingly provides false or misleading material information to:
  > (a) an officer of the court for the purpose of influencing a criminal proceeding;

- *76-8-506 Providing false information to law enforcement officers, government agencies, or specified professionals.*
  A person is guilty of a class B misdemeanor if he:

(1) knowingly gives or causes to be given false information to any peace officer or any state or local government agency or personnel with a purpose of inducing the recipient of the information to believe that another has committed an offense;

- *76-8-510.5 Tampering with evidence — Definitions — Elements — Penalties.*
  (1) As used in this section, "thing or item" includes any document, record book, paper, file, electronic compilation, or other evidence.
  (2) A person is guilty of tampering with evidence if, believing that an official proceeding or investigation is pending or about to be instituted, or with the intent to prevent an official proceeding or investigation or to prevent the production of any thing or item which reasonably would be anticipated to be evidence in the official proceeding or investigation, the person knowingly or intentionally:

  > (a) alters, destroys, conceals, or removes any thing or item with the purpose of impairing the veracity or availability of the thing or item in the proceeding or investigation; or
  > (b) makes, presents, or uses any thing or item which the person knows to be false with the purpose of deceiving a public servant or any other party who is or may be engaged in the proceeding or investigation.

- *76-8-511 Falsification or alteration of government record — Penalty.*
  A person is guilty of a class B misdemeanor if under circumstances not amounting to an offense subject to a greater penalty under Title 76, Chapter 6, Part 5, Fraud, the person:

(1) knowingly makes a false entry in or false alteration of anything belonging to, received, or kept by the government for information or record, or required by law to be kept for information of the government;

- *18 U.S. Code § 241 - Conspiracy against rights*
  If two or more persons conspire to injure, oppress, threaten, or intimidate any person in any State, Territory, Commonwealth, Possession, or District in the free exercise or enjoyment of any right or privilege secured to him by the Constitution or laws of the United States, or because of his having so exercised the same; [t]hey shall be fined under this title or imprisoned not more than ten years, or both;

Just because the syndicate chooses not to police itself does not in any way, shape, or form diminish the fact that the individuals involved in the conspiracy reported in this chapter are criminals. All the miscreants mentioned are criminals, and that's the end of it. Ironically, the one who was charged with a crime is the only non-criminal. This is often standard operating procedure for the syndicate.

Background

The criminal case against Mr. Sanchez stemmed from a charge alleging that he had failed to stop at the command of a police officer. On an early December morning of 2014, police had been dispatched to a residence where a party had taken place and a fight had been reported. When police arrived, Mr. Sanchez and multiple other people in different vehicles were in the process of driving away.

One responding officer was Jared Brooks Cardon from the Unified Police Department of Greater Salt Lake. In his police report, Officer Cardon stated that once he arrived near the residence, he saw three vehicles getting ready to leave. Officer Cardon then stated that he stepped out of his patrol vehicle and stretched his arms out and signaled the vehicle closest to him to stop.

Court records from an evidentiary hearing offer testimony in which Sanchez declared he was the second vehicle in line. Sanchez as well as Cardon stated that the first vehicle in line had stopped once Cardon gestured for it to stop. Both Sanchez and Cardon then declared that the first car in line drove around the officer and accelerated away.

Next is when the issue arises. Officer Jared Cardon claims that Luis Sanchez was driving the first car in line. He also stated that he slammed his hand on the hood of Sanchez's car in an effort to order him to stop. Mr. Sanchez and multiple other witnesses affirm that Sanchez was the second car in line and that they never saw any officer slam the hood of Sanchez's car nor any other vehicle that was about to drive away.

Sanchez maintains he was never given a direct order to stop. He said that he only drove away after waiting a significant amount of time after Cardon ran into his patrol vehicle after the first car had driven away. Believing they were not being sought by police, Sanchez and the other vehicle behind him resumed driving.

Cardon refutes this and claims that the first car in line was that of Sanchez. He alleges that Sanchez willfully ignored numerous commands to stop and that he drove away while the other two vehicles waited. He explained that the blatant disregard of his commands to stop led him to charge Sanchez with fleeing and then subsequently with DUI and resisting arrest. Cardon's version of events and the order of the vehicles is heavily contradicted through court testimony and by multiple witnesses.

In March of 2017, after hearing the testimony of multiple witnesses concerning the arrest and specifically the order of the vehicles, Judge Bruce Lubeck determined that "the second vehicle, a Toyota Camry, was driven by Defendant." Judge Lubeck was convinced that Mr. Sanchez was the second car in line when Cardon approached the scene. Nonetheless, the case and the charges against Sanchez continued.

Throughout the proceeding, Sanchez was persistent in attempting to acquire police dashboard camera and police station recordings because he believed he could prove that Cardon was lying about what really occurred the morning of his arrest. Sanchez was convinced dashboard camera footage would prove he did not flee or resist arrest and that he was not impaired to drive because he says that he had performed all field sobriety tests and completed them successfully.

Officer Cardon declared in a court hearing that Sanchez only took one field sobriety test and refused further testing. At another hearing, he declared that Sanchez took and completed all tests but failed them all. At yet another hearing, he stated he did not remember if Sanchez completed them. Cardon heavily contradicted his own testimony throughout the case. Video recordings of the arrest would have clarified what truly occurred.

The case had been pending for five years, and the Unified Police Department failed to provide any videos regarding the arrest. Department officers claim that the dashboard camera recordings of the vehicles were never saved due to a system malfunction and that the recordings from the police department were ultimately deleted.

Destruction of exculpatory evidence was a clear violation of Sanchez's constitutional right to due process. The state is required to retain and provide any exculpatory evidence that was ever in its possession and that may help a defendant with his case. Due to the destruction of this evidence, Sanchez was not afforded the opportunity to adequately defend himself against the state and its actors. If Heather Chesnut and Daniel Torrence would have brought this constitutional violation to the attention of the court, it could have forced the prosecutor to dismiss the charges against Sanchez.

Chesnut and Torrence not only failed to represent Sanchez adequately, but they also used the criminal justice system to punish him for attempting to exercise his constitutional right to a jury trial. In effect, they said, "How dare Mr. Sanchez ask for a jury trial!"—a right granted him under the U.S. Constitution.

Despite constant pressure from his attorneys to plead guilty, Sanchez remained determined to go to trial. His unwavering determination angered Chesnut and Torrence. This meant they would have to spend time preparing the case for trial and subsequently attend the trial, which, by the way, is part of their job.

Sanchez stated that at one meeting, Chesnut asked him why he wanted to go to trial and become a felon for the fleeing charge. She asked him if he was trying to get initiated into a gang and told him that she believed this was the only reason he would want to go to trial. Sanchez replied that he did not want to plead guilty for something he did not do.

On the morning of March 19, 2018, Chesnut and Torrence conspired with others to put their own client in jail for challenging his charges and refusing to plead guilty. They are now being sued. Their client Luis Sanchez had been claiming his innocence since the inception of the criminal case and had demanded a jury trial. He had also made multiple unsuccessful requests to have crucial video evidence released to him concerning his arrest.

For years his defense attorneys had been pressuring him to plead guilty without ever receiving or reviewing video evidence that police had in their possession. Sanchez felt so frustrated by the lack of assistance from his primary attorney, Heather Chesnut, that he was forced to file his own legal motions.

Conspiring Against their Own Client

On March 19th, 2018, Sanchez was scheduled to appear for a pretrial conference at 9 a.m., but Chesnut and Torrence had a different plan. They conspired to have a warrant issued against their own client by having his case called early and before he was supposed to be in court. This was all caught by courtroom audio and video recordings and is shown at www.oais.us/sanchez.php. This video will be referenced hereafter in this chapter as follows: (xx:yy), wherein the parenthetical time indicates the elapsed time of the video itself when the statement or action being referenced begins.

In the video, Torrence is heard whispering to Chesnut, "Let's call it and get a warrant," and then laughs. Chesnut points to the clock on the wall (00:22). The time at the courthouse is 8:39 a.m. Sanchez and dozens of other individuals are not scheduled for court for another twenty-one minutes.

"Is it time?" Torrence asks Chesnut. "8:40? Ok. Four Minutes? 8:45" (00:36). Five minutes pass and Chesnut tells the judge they are ready to proceed on Sanchez's case. It is 8:45 a.m., and the prosecutor walks over to address the court and participate in the scheme (00:57).

Attorneys and Judge—Corruption at the Highest Level

Torrence gets up from the attorney's table and calls for Sanchez as he overtly scans the courtroom to search for him (01:18). He doesn't see Sanchez, shrugs, and immediately turns and looks at prosecutor Nathanael Swift. Swift, right on cue, mutters, "But he always comes in late" (01:31).

Judge Katherine Bernards-Goodman calls Sanchez's case and asks Chesnut and Torrence whether they are expecting Sanchez to arrive. She is aware of the time and that court hearings are not supposed to start for another 15 minutes (01:44).

Torrence explains, "I always expect him, although last time he was not here, and it was only after my secretary called him that he remembered to come" (01:55). Court documents show that at the previous court hearing, Torrence failed to appear for the scheduled pretrial conference and Judge Bernards-Goodman thus rescheduled it. Torrence's statement was nothing but a deliberate and false accusation against his own client.

Prosecutor Swift then states, "Mr. Sanchez has a history of coming in very late. He has missed a few altogether" (02:14). Court records indicate that Mr. Sanchez had been late to court once and that he had missed two court hearings in the span of five years for which the case had been pending. In one of the missed court hearings, Sanchez's bond company called the court explaining that they had given Sanchez the wrong court date.

It was clear to the judge what was taking place: a concerted plan by both defense attorneys and the prosecutor to have a warrant issued against Sanchez for failing to appear. Bernards-Goodman proceeds to order a $15,000 cash-only warrant against Sanchez (02:57). A cash-only warrant meant that Sanchez would not be able to seek the services of a bail bond company. The full bail amount would be required to be paid in cash in exchange for his release.

Once the warrant was ordered, the court clerk asked Bernards-Goodman, "So, what are we going to do when he shows up" (03:05)?

Bernards-Goodman then replied, "We're going to take him into custody," and laughed about it (03:08).

Sanchez Enters the Lion's Den

During an interview given to *The Salt Lake Tribune*, Sanchez told reporter Jessica Miller that at the hearing of March 19th, 2018, he had arrived early to court. He said he spent a few minutes waiting in his car to kill time before entering the courthouse.

Sanchez stated he was outside the courtroom doors by 9 a.m. He also claims he attempted to walk inside, but the courtroom was overcrowded. This is evident from courtroom video footage. Sanchez said he waited outside the courtroom for it to empty partially before he attempted to find a seat. He explained he did not go inside because he had many times been instructed to wait outside and not block the doors since it was a "safety hazard."

At 9:07 a.m., the courtroom had partially emptied, and Sanchez entered (03:33). A few minutes later, the courtroom was again overflowing, and bailiff Steve Adams instructed people to go outside. At 9:17 a.m., Sanchez walks up to Chesnut and asks her where Torrence is. She informs him that his case had been called and that a warrant had been issued for his arrest. She instructs him to wait until his case is once again called by the judge. In the video, prosecutor Swift can be seen looking directly at Chesnut and Sanchez while they are speaking (04:10).

Sanchez then waits for over an hour and one-half before prosecutor Nathanael Swift finally decides to tell the judge that Sanchez is present (05:00). Bernards-Goodman replies by saying, "And we're going to execute the warrant," and then laughs about it (05:33). She finds amusement in what is taking place and what they are about to do.

While Mr. Sanchez is being handcuffed, Bernards-Goodman jokes, "He's good at what he does. He doesn't ask until he's between him and the door" (06:18). At this point, Sanchez is led through and out of the courtroom. Discussion ensues in the courtroom, and Bernards-Goodman questions the other criminals, "So, maybe we should call it so that we can document what time he came in" (07:17).

When Sanchez is later led back into the courtroom, discussion ensues between him and Bernards-Goodman. Regarding the time the syndicate wants the record to reflect, she says, "Well, you did not come to our courtroom until a quarter to eleven" (08:03). This is a blatant lie. Mr. Sanchez then asks when the arrest warrant was issued (08:51). Bernards-Goodman lies unabashedly for at least the second time, "But we didn't issue it until after nine. And you're here way after that" (08:58). The video clearly shows them conspiring earlier that morning before the hearing was scheduled. Again, see the court minutes in the appendix to verify that the pretrial conference was supposed to begin at 9:00 a.m.

A couple of important things need to be noted:

- Until he was able to produce bail, Mr. Sanchez had to spend almost two weeks in jail, which is exactly almost two weeks too long.

- Whoever edited the video forgot to put the prefix "dis" before the word "honorable" in front of Bernards-Goodman's name (9:22).

Assault on the People

What happened to Mr. Sanchez was not only an assault on him; more significantly, it was an assault on the people. When people lose faith in their judicial system, it puts the very fabric of our society in jeopardy.

After all, why would people willingly walk into a courtroom to fight a battle if they know they have no chance at a fair trial or due process—wherein government personnel in an entire courtroom are willing to act with complete disregard of the law and without any consequences?

As of March 2021, there had been no consequences to any of the perpetrators. Judge Bernards-Goodman retired with full benefits. Prosecutor Swift still holds his position. The Salt Lake Legal Defender Association zealously defended the actions of Chesnut and Torrence. The Unified Police Department keeps violating people's constitutional rights. Nothing has changed since the inception of Sanchez's case. Nothing corrective or punitive has been done even after irrefutable video evidence revealed the systemic corruption within the injustice system in Utah and complaints were filed against the judge and lawyers with the respective oversight boards.

Corruption within the entire Utah judicial system was necessary in order for the events in Luis Sanchez's case to transpire. From false reports and deliberate withholding and destruction of evidence by the police to an entire courtroom participating in the unlawful arrest of Sanchez, the full spectrum of the syndicate had to operate in unison. Clearly, the criminals involved did not have the faintest interest in justice.[6]

It is truly revolting what Mr. Sanchez had to endure—and is still enduring—with regard to a completely contrived criminal case. Note that it spawned other legal battles for him, which, of course, is by design. The injustice system feeds on others' misfortune, which is oftentimes a direct result of the syndicate's own actions. And the more misfortune, the more it eats. If one example isn't enough to demonstrate just how polluted the toxic waste dump really is, another equally astounding example is given in the next chapter.

Chapter 6: My Experience with the Syndicate

Everything faded into mist. The past was erased, the erasure was forgotten, the lie became truth. — **George Orwell, *1984***

TRASH FOUND IN THE TOXIC WASTE DUMP

The waste materials—some more toxic and dangerous than others—named in the following subsections are a subset of the many miscreants I have encountered during my interactions with the U.S. injustice system over the last two decades. Many of them belong in prison. Only one of them, Alyssa L. Parent, is not part of the system, but all of the others are either lawyers or glorified unelected lawyers in black gowns. But for her, their roles in the wrongdoing that served as a conduit for the injustice I have suffered at the hands of the syndicate will be explained further in the second section of this chapter. In order to minimize superscripting and endnotes, evidence for this chapter can be found by visiting the following link: www.stloiyf.com/complaint/complaint.htm.

Alyssa L. Parent

Parent is the person who refused to pay approximately $4,300 for my consulting and HVAC services. In conjunction with a prior attorney of hers, Joseph L. Michaud, they lied repeatedly in many court papers and proceedings and obtained a fraudulent court judgment in the civil case that was filed in the People's Republic of Massachusetts by a collections attorney I hired to pursue the matter. Through another attorney, Douglas H. Smith, she filed the fraudulent judgment in Rhode Island in order to attach property I no longer own there.

Joseph L. Michaud

A former attorney in Massachusetts who was recently appointed judge in 2018, Michaud represented Parent in the civil case described in the previous subsection and committed multiple violations of rules of procedure, civil and criminal laws, and the U.S. Constitution. He has repeatedly conspired to steer court proceedings in the direction he wanted them to go. He has been sued several times in unrelated matters. Without question, he does not belong on the bench but instead belongs behind bars.

Kevan J. Cunningham

When the aforementioned civil case was at the trial level, Cunningham presided over the majority of it. He ruled contrary to law and violated many court rules of procedure. This is the same judge who managed to escape indictment and conviction in the RICO case brought by federal officials in the summer of 2014.

Several Other State Judges

As the same civil case made its way through all levels of the appellate courts in Massachusetts, it got rubber-stamped by other state judges who were equally culpable: Kathryn E. Hand, Kevin J. Finnerty, Ariane D. Vuono, Mary T. Sullivan, Gregory I. Massing, and the late Ralph D. Gants.

Douglas H. Smith

Smith is the attorney who represents Parent as of this writing. He is trying to steal for his client property in Rhode Island that he knows was levied based on a fraudulent judgment issued against me in Massachusetts. He brought the case into the Rhode Island court system and did not withdraw the matter once he understood that I no longer own the property or once he learned about the facts of the originating judgment—that he now knows is fraudulent.

Nelson F. Brinckerhoff

After the fraudulent judgment that was issued against me by the Massachusetts courts was then later recorded in the Rhode Island courts, I paid Brinckerhoff to attend a court hearing on my behalf since I could not feasibly attend myself. At the eleventh hour, just a couple days before the hearing, he changed his mind and said he would not be attending it and also decided to keep the money I paid him specifically for that purpose. I have therefore been forced to sue him in small claims court.

Kristin Tavia Mihelic

Mihelic works as an attorney for the Department of Injustice. From the very beginning of my bankruptcy, she intended to block the discharge of a "debt" attributed to me that was obtained fraudulently as a result of the aforementioned civil case involving Parent and Michaud in Massachusetts. To do this, Mihelic filed a baseless civil complaint against me in federal court as a favor to Michaud. She has lied dozens of times; violated legal ethics, rules of procedure, civil and criminal laws, and the U.S. Constitution; and shown by her actions that she also belongs in the black bar hotel.

Lies Told

Mihelic is a pathological liar and epitomizes the joke, "How can you tell when a lawyer is lying? When her lips move." However, with her the following should be appended: "or when she writes any legal document." She has spewed the following lies, which are not intended to constitute an exhaustive list.

She lied regarding dollar amounts listed in my bankruptcy schedules. She also lied regarding certain statements I made that pertain to documents filed and properties that I manage. Prior to a meeting, I did not provide "only two documents" as she stated. I actually provided five by email.

Mihelic refused both in a subpoena and in a request for production to provide phone records that I requested simply containing "number and duration of each call"—not any particular *content* of the calls or anything regarding "information and records that are protected by the attorney work product and attorney-client privileges" as she falsely stated. The reason I only asked for general information in the subpoena and in the request for production is that I knew private information could legitimately be blocked.

She and the court had no legal authority to block me from receiving a mere listing of phone numbers and duration of calls. The fact that such records exist is not protected, which she definitely knows. By blocking me, which I fully expected to happen, the proverbial smoking gun was exposed.

Particularly of note with regard to Mihelic lying that she did not communicate with Michaud are the 341 meetings. When they were being held, I noticed that no other petitioners were being questioned by U.S. government trial attorneys. The only petitioner *two* people—a private trustee and a government trial attorney for the U.S. trustee—were questioning was me. Afterward, I emailed the private trustee and asked, "How often does a trial attorney from the government attend the 341 meetings?"

He confirmed my suspicion by effectively saying it almost never happens when he replied, "Not very often." In fact, I asked other private trustees in different regions the same question, but they didn't even bother to respond at all—apparently thinking the question I asked was so alien that it didn't deserve a reply.

If still not convinced that Mihelic had been contacted by Michaud, conspired with him to block the discharge, and then lied about it, consider the following. Well over a year after I initially filed complaints with the Office of the Inspector General and Office of "Professional" Responsibility, which as of December 2020 I began doing occasionally but as of January 2022 I now do daily, I finally received an electronic letter in February 2022 from the OIG. It stated, "This Office's jurisdiction to investigate allegations of misconduct by a private trustee is very limited.....We have forwarded your correspondence .....Of course, if you have information that involves

.....issues regarding DOJ employees.....please feel free to submit that information to us."

The assumption by the OIG that my complaint was filed against a private trustee and not a government trial attorney for the U.S. trustee is telling. It is so incredibly rare for such an attorney to attend 341 meetings that the OIG automatically assumed my complaint was against the private trustee even though I have always included Mihelic's name and government email address on the online form. With respect to the stacks of evidence provided already, it is abundantly clear that Michaud contacted Mihelic, committed more crimes, and interfered with justice, and Mihelic followed suit.

In one particular email to me, Mihelic said, "The depositions are required to be conducted during regular business hours," but no such rule or law exists. In fact, rule 7029 of the Federal Rules of Bankruptcy Procedure says the exact opposite—that depositions can take place "at any time."

Mihelic said that "the parties are required to meet and confer in an attempt to resolve discovery disputes." This is also not true. She said this many times. Rules of court only require such meetings at the initial pre-trial hearing and other specific times, not during discovery.

During discovery, I asked Mihelic to provide certain records of telephonic and other communication to and from attorneys and others in Massachusetts and Rhode Island. One in particular was Attorney Douglas H. Smith. Recall that he is the attorney in Rhode Island who is trying to collect on a fraudulent foreign judgment issued by the Massachusetts courts. In addition to objecting, she stated "no such documents exist" in one of her responses, which contradicts the evidence she inadvertently provided and that was buried in more than 500 pages of photocopied email transmissions. It also contradicts evidence provided by Attorney Nelson Brinckerhoff, the attorney in another related matter, who made a statement providing further proof that Attorney Smith communicated with Mihelic. Rest assured that *unredacted* phone records, if they could be obtained, would additionally prove the communication(s).

Mihelic also withheld evidence that she communicated with Michaud because she did so early in the matter, probably within the first couple weeks of my bankruptcy filing, when he contacted her and asked her to block my bankruptcy as a favor to him. I know a call was made and state this not only based on the evidence presented regarding the subpoena above, but also because all "creditors" except for the *only one* I listed as part of my petition have gone kicking and screaming to prevent the discharge, filing document after document with the court. The only problem with their claims is that they have me mixed up with another person who has a name similar to mine. I do not know these entities and owe no debts to them or to anyone else, in fact.

The only entity that has *not* made an appearance in the chapter 7 case is the party who obtained the fraudulent judgment in Massachusetts, Alyssa L. Parent. She is the *only* "creditor" I listed in my original petition—and who is attempting to attach property I no longer own in Rhode Island. Michaud, who believes he is untouchable because of the power he now wields as a judge, likely told attorney Smith, "Don't waste your time and money filing anything with the court. I will make a call and take care of this." After at least four calls to my previous attorneys whereby he violated Massachusetts criminal law chapter 268 § 13B(1)(c)(v), it is obvious that this is his *modus operandi.*

Mihelic made an absolutely ludicrous statement when she said I "provided only a general denial at best" of the fraud and corruption underlying the original fraudulent judgment. I provided mountains of evidence of corruption, fraud, and other criminal acts, including, but not limited to, the evidence offered to her in an email, the open letter to the court and her, and the initial disclosures sent by email.

I have essentially been shouting from the rooftops since the beginning of my bankruptcy that *the judgment issued in Massachusetts is fraudulent* .....because it is! It is just that Mihelic ignored the evidence, particularly in all her documents, so later appeals courts and/or oversight boards could be duped into believing her lies and also enticed into ignoring the evidence. By doing so, she went completely against the grain of Rule 11(b)(4) of the Federal Rules of Civil Procedure, which states "the denials of factual contentions are warranted on the evidence or, if specifically so identified, are reasonably based on belief or a lack of information."

Mihelic also repeatedly stated that I "failed to timely or substantially communicate with the [p]laintiff regarding same." What she meant to say is that I failed to communicate *over the phone* so that she could hide her lies because there would be no irrefutable physical record of them and limit the damage I could do to her in court papers and especially in complaints outside of court.

In one particular motion, Mihelic said, "The [d]efendant failed to cooperate with the [A]UST in scheduling his deposition." She continued, "the [d]efendant failed to provide a reasonable time when his deposition could be conducted," and, "Despite numerous requests from the [A]UST that he identify dates where he could start the deposition during normal business hours, the [d]efendant refused to do so." These statements are completely untrue as can be seen from examining the facts and evidence. I provided dates and times, some during "normal business hours."

Lastly, in Mihelic's motion to extend time to file, she once again proudly touted another untruth in an extremely long line of lies. She stated, "The [d]efendant filed his [o]bjection to the [m]otion on March 4, 2021 (Docket No. 118). The [d]efendant's filing was one day late." I filed my objection on March 3, 2021, and within the deadline, not on March 4, 2021, as she falsely claimed. I contacted the court clerk after I noticed a $10 discrepancy. The clerk said in an email, "Always good to file accurate documents. Please file an amended copy and explain what is amended." On March 4, 2021, I filed an amended copy as per the clerk's direction. Mihelic later contradicted herself when she declared in a separate pleading that I filed my objection "on March 3, 2021." Since the pleading was signed "under penalty of perjury" and it is replete with incorrect dates and untruthful statements and it contains a clear contradiction, she committed perjury.

One false statement in a legal proceeding could be considered a mistake. More than two (and certainly well in excess of thirty) is clearly a concerted effort to stymie and mislead. There are many other instances, but I omitted them in the interest of brevity. It should be apparent by now that Mihelic's habitual lying is uncontrollable.

Deliberately Choosing to Be a Party to Fraud

Mihelic has repeatedly denied—or, at the very least, completely failed to investigate—the existence of rampant fraud and corruption related to the fraudulent Massachusetts court judgment underlying my chapter 7 filing, which is in itself a form of fraud for which she is solely responsible. I not only told her in several bankruptcy meetings that the judgment entered against me in Rhode Island is fraudulent but also offered in an email to provide plenty of irrefutable evidence. She never accepted that offer. Instead of fighting the fraud, she fought against me in order to *perpetuate* the fraud.

I called the Department of Injustice and the Federal Bureau of Iniquity for nearly thirty days straight sometime near the end of 2017 after previously filing multiple times with these agencies criminal complaints against the responsible individuals. What was the result? Nobody lifted a toxic finger to help. I also offered to provide a copy of one of the complaints to Mihelic, but, not surprisingly, she showed no interest in receiving it.

Violations of California Business and Professions Code Section 6068

With regard to section (a) of this law, Mihelic disregarded the Constitution by violating my right of due process under the Fifth Amendment. Additionally, she exceeded the "look back" period—and sometimes by large amounts—in most of her discovery requests and in other facets of the case. With regard to section (c) that she "maintain those actions, proceedings, or defenses only as appear to him or her legal or just," she is pursuing her meritless case against me only to double down in order to protect her associates and conceal the true fraud and corruption in the matter. With regard to section (d), employing "for the purpose of maintaining the causes confided to him or her, those means only as are consistent with truth," she has failed miserably. Her violation of section (g), that she not "encourage either the commencement or the continuance of an action or proceeding from any corrupt motive of passion or interest," is perhaps the biggest of this particular law since her motives are corrupt.

Perjury

Perjury is governed generally by 18 U.S. Code § 1621. Mihelic perjured herself as explained in the Lies Told subsection above and has therefore violated this federal law. 18 U.S. Code § 1623 is a perjury statute that she likewise violated because she lied at least a dozen times in several sworn declarations. She is also guilty of other crimes, some of which are proved in the following subsections.

Misprision of Felony

18 U.S. Code § 4 states, "Whoever, having knowledge of the actual commission of a felony cognizable by a court of the United States, conceals and does not as soon as possible make known the same to some judge or other person in civil or military authority under the United States, shall be fined under this title or imprisoned not more than three years, or both." As stated previously, Mihelic was made fully aware of felonious acts committed by others, which caused my chapter 7 bankruptcy. Since she has concealed such felonies, she has broken this criminal law.

Destruction, Alteration, or Falsification of Records in Federal Investigations and Bankruptcy

18 U.S. Code § 1519 says in part, "Whoever knowingly.....conceals, covers up, falsifies, or makes a false entry in any record, document.....with the intent to impede, obstruct, or influence the investigation or proper administration of any matter.....or any case filed under title 11....." Mihelic concealed or, at the very least, tried to conceal fraud and corruption by ignoring my related statements in the 341 meetings and also in the email I sent her on May 13, 2020, indicating that I have more than enough documents that reveal the true fraud and corruption in the underlying matter in Massachusetts. She has also falsified many records.

Fraud/Conspiracy to Commit Fraud

18 U.S. Code § 1001 specifically says in provisions one and three,

> ".....whoever.....knowingly and willfully—
>
> (1) falsifies, conceals, or covers up by any trick, scheme, or device a material fact;
>
> (3) makes or uses any false writing or document knowing the same to contain any materially false, fictitious, or fraudulent statement or entry;
>
> shall be fined under this title, imprisoned not more than 5 years....."

Provision one was violated through the cover up of fraud in Massachusetts and the communication Mihelic had with Smith and Michaud. Provision three was violated because she knowingly used a fraudulent judgment as the basis for her case, because of the false answer(s) she gave in her response to my request for production of documents as previously stated, and because every single known document she has filed with the court has contained materially false, fictitious, or fraudulent statements. 18 U.S. Code § 1018 was also violated for the foregoing latter reason. 18 U.S. Code § 1341 addresses "any scheme or artifice to defraud"—in which Mihelic has participated. 18 U.S. Code § 1349 concerns conspiracy to commit fraud. If she is involved with Michaud or any others in perpetuating this whole charade, then she has violated this criminal law.

Concealment of Assets; False Oaths and Claims; Bribery

18 U.S. Code § 152 specifically says in provisions two and three,

> "A person who—
>
> (2) knowingly and fraudulently makes a false oath or account in or in relation to any case under title 11;
>
> (3) knowingly and fraudulently makes a false declaration, certificate, verification, or statement under penalty of perjury as permitted under section 1746 of title 28, in or in relation to any case under title 11;
>
> shall be fined under this title, imprisoned not more than 5 years, or both."

These provisions were violated when Mihelic perjured herself, when she performed the acts proved in the Lies Told subsection above, and at other times.

Bankruptcy Investigations

18 U.S. Code § 3057 specifically says in subsection (a):

> "Any judge, receiver, or trustee having reasonable grounds for believing that any violation under chapter 9 of this title or other laws of the United States relating to insolvent debtors, receiverships or reorganization plans has been committed, or that an investigation should be had in connection therewith, shall report to the appropriate United States attorney all the facts and circumstances of the case, the names of the witnesses and the offense or

offenses believed to have been committed. Where one of such officers has made such report, the others need not do so."

This subsection was violated when Mihelic refused to report to a U.S. attorney the underlying crimes that gave rise to my bankruptcy as explained throughout this section and specifically in the Lies Told subsection above.

Tiffany Louise Carroll

As the acting U.S. trustee for my bankruptcy, Carroll's job was to oversee all the activities happening in the matter and ensure rules and laws were followed. Instead, she let Mihelic do whatever she pleased. English philosopher John Stuart Mill in the 1860s wrote, "Bad [wo]men need nothing more to compass their ends, than that good [wo]men should look on and do nothing." Anyone who merely looks on is therefore not truly good and is certainly at least partially responsible. Accordingly, Carroll has been named with Mihelic and Louise DeCarl Adler in a lawsuit I was forced to file against the three as mentioned in the second to last paragraph of this chapter.

Louise DeCarl Adler

Alder is the judge who presided over my bankruptcy case and, while doing so, disregarded rules of court, the law, and the U.S. Constitution. She also lied multiple times and violated the Code of Conduct for United States Judges. Moving real property out of harm's way, of which I was falsely accused, is exactly what this hypocrite-criminal did. She did this the day after I informed her that I would be publicly attacking her character by posting online reviews in order to ensure that she would never again rent her condominiums to anyone. The irony of it all is that they are located at 666 Upas Street, San Diego, California. As the saying on the street goes, one can't make this sh!t up.

There are some major red flags concerning Judge Adler's actions. When viewed out of context and individually, they may not seem significant. However, when viewed together in the grand scheme of things, it is *highly* unlikely that she performed her judicial duties objectively and without some sort of connection to the criminal activity of Mihelic and certain individuals in Massachusetts and Rhode Island. All I ask when I go into *any* court in this country is that members of the syndicate follow their own rules and laws. I have been before no fewer than seventy judges in my life and can count the times on one hand that they have.

A judge is supposed to uphold the law, not be its biggest violator. Undoubtedly, Judge Adler has violated the Code of Conduct for United States Judges, rules of court, civil and criminal statutory law, *stare decisis*, and the U.S. Constitution. These violations are proved in the following subsections.

Violation of 28 U.S. Code § 1930 (f)(1)

When my bankruptcy was initially filed, Judge Adler seemed to be deliberately steering the case in the direction she wanted it to go. She tried to block me from filing my chapter 7 petition in the first place by not allowing me to proceed *in forma pauperis* and making me pay the filing fee. However, since the date on which I filed my Chapter 7 petition, I have requested a fee waiver eight other times, and *all eight* have been unconditionally granted—two of which were for the related "financial management courses" that are required as part of the bankruptcy process. In all instances, I provided the *same* financial information, so her decision is extremely suspicious. The obvious reason why I was blocked from filing without paying the filing fee when the fee was waived in all eight other instances is that someone in government who is associated with my bankruptcy received a phone call from Michaud asking that person to deny my petition.

Not Abiding by *Stare Decisis* with Respect to Information Not Protect by Attorney-Client Privilege

Judge Adler also allowed Mihelic's motion to quash my subpoena to produce phone records strictly comprised of number, date/time, and duration of each call—not any particular *content* of the calls or anything else. The command in my subpoena was not something that could be even remotely misconstrued as telling Mihelic to provide "information and records that are protected by the attorney work product and attorney-client privileges." This is nonsense. During discovery I requested the same phone records, which Mihelic again refused to provide.

As stated previously, the reason I just asked for general information in the subpoena is that I knew private information could legitimately be blocked. Judge Adler had no legal authority to prevent me from receiving a mere listing of phone numbers and duration of calls. The act of her—and Mihelic—blocking me, which I fully expected to happen, is a strong indicator that communication between Adler and Michaud and/or Michaud and Mihelic occurred.

As explained in the Lies Told subsection above, the fact that such records exist is not protected, which Judge Adler and Mihelic know full well. In conjunction with the information presented in that same subjection regarding records of communications I requested during discovery, there is now no question that calls were made by and/or to Michaud and that he contaminated the instant case by his own false statements. It is a virtual guarantee.

Not Abiding by *Stare Decisis* with Respect to Illegally Denying a Jury Trial

Mihelic filed a motion to deny my right to a jury trial. Judge Alder allowed the motion even though ample supporting statutory and case law I cited says she should have denied it—probably because she does not read anything I submit to the court. During the December 17, 2020, telephonic conference, Adler did not respond to me after I firmly asked, "Are you reading anything I send you?" Instead, I was met with dead silence, which confirms that she doesn't.

I was especially careful in my answer to Mihelic's complaint not to file a counterclaim because *Granfinanciera, S.A. v. Nordberg*, 492 U.S. 33 (1989), said that a defendant who files a counterclaim in a bankruptcy proceeding is deemed to have consented to the bankruptcy court's jurisdiction and waived any right to a jury trial. That court also said a litigant has a right to a jury trial when the cause of action is legal in nature and when it concerns private rights. In my answer, I simply asked for "punitive damages from AUST and the U.S. government, plus attorney fees, costs, and interest," which are legal in nature.

McCord v. Papantoniou, 316 B.R. 113 (E.D.N.Y. 2004), which I cited in a motion I filed in the bankruptcy court and concerned fraudulent conveyance, made clear that "the defendant's right to a jury trial is preserved where both legal and equitable claims are asserted." Relevant law is also found in the U.S. Supreme Court case *Curtis v. Loether*, 415 U.S. 189 (1974), which I also cited in the same motion: "More important, the relief sought here—actual and punitive damages—is the traditional form of relief offered in the courts of law." Footnote 11 of that matter also lends it help by stating, "If the action is properly viewed as one for damages only, our conclusion that this is a legal claim obviously requires a jury trial on demand. And if this legal claim is joined with an equitable claim, the right to jury trial on the legal claim, including all issues common to both claims, remains intact." A plethora of additional supporting law validates my right to the jury trial I was denied.

Not Abiding by *Stare Decisis* Regarding Appointment of Counsel

28 U.S. Code § 1915(e)(1) says, "The court may request an attorney to represent any person unable to afford counsel." The decision is generally discretionary except in two types of proceedings, one of which involves indigent people being potentially deprived of their right against self-incrimination as

protected by the Fifth Amendment or being potentially deprived of that same right as protected by the Fourteenth Amendment through due process. Appointed counsel is required for indigent litigants whenever rights against self-incrimination are imperiled, regardless of the situation.

The U.S. Supreme Court opined in *Maness v. Meyers*, 419 U.S. 449 (1975), "This Court has always broadly construed [Fifth Amendment privilege against self-incrimination] protection to assure that an individual is not compelled to produce evidence which later may be used against him as an accused in a criminal action." Continuing in its opinion, it said that "counsel must be appointed for any indigent witness, whether or not he is a party, in any proceeding in which his testimony can be compelled.....Unless counsel is appointed, these indigents will be deprived, just as surely as Maness' client would have been had he not been advised by Maness, of the opportunity to decide whether to assert their constitutional privilege." Bear in mind that the high court's decision was not split; it was *unanimous*.

During a phone conference, Judge Adler upheld her tentative ruling issued earlier to compel discovery, including deposing me. After I informed her of 28 U.S. Code § 1915(e)(1) by quoting it directly and of the unanimous *Maness* ruling, she failed to acknowledge that the law allows for appointed counsel outside of criminal proceedings and actually mandated it in the adversary case created by Mihelic in my bankruptcy. Adler said I would only be represented by appointed counsel if "the U.S. trustee finds that [I] made false statements" in the case and

I am charged criminally. Notice that she mentioned nothing regarding the statements being alleged until proved in court and thus completely disregarded due process. The word of Mihelic would itself be sufficient to substantiate the veracity of such statements. This is nothing less than horrifying.

That aside, the intent of *Maness* is *preventative*, not *reparative*, so her "reasoning" was wrong. That court stated, "Although the proceeding in which he is called is not criminal, it is established that a witness may not be required to answer a question if there is some rational basis for believing that it will incriminate him, at least without at that time being assured that neither it nor its fruits may be used against him."

In the same phone conference, Judge Adler asked, "Have you tried legal aid?"

I replied, "Yes, but nobody will touch it. There's too much corruption."

Instead of replying, "Oh my, well, we will investigate that, and, yes, I will abide by the law and Constitution and appoint you counsel," she said, "Well, I can't help you."

Misprision of Felony

As stated previously, just as Mihelic was apprised of felonious acts committed by others, so was Judge Adler. I sent an open letter to the court informing her of such acts. I told her many times verbally and in court filings that Mihelic committed perjury and other misconduct, upon which Adler failed to act (correctively). Since she has also concealed the felonies committed by others—who now include

Mihelic—she has violated criminal law 18 U.S. Code § 4 too and is an accessory after the fact.

Destruction, Alteration, or Falsification of Records in Federal Investigations and Bankruptcy

Judge Adler, as has Mihelic, has concealed or, at the very least, tried to conceal fraud and corruption by ignoring the open letter I submitted to the court and all the records that reveal the true fraud and corruption in the underlying matter in Massachusetts. Thus, she has also broken criminal law 18 U.S. Code § 1519.

Bankruptcy Investigations

Judge Adler, as has Mihelic, has violated 18 U.S. Code § 3057, the law associated with this subsection, because she refused to report to a U.S. attorney the same underlying matters that Mihelic failed to report and then compounded the violation by refusing to report Mihelic for her misconduct and crimes.

Actions Completely Wrong and Completely Illegal

The crimes that have been committed against me by the syndicate in California are no different from the ones in prior cases in Massachusetts: perjury, misprision of felony, fraud, conspiracy to commit fraud, obstruction of justice, and falsifying evidence, records, and documents. Nothing has changed; the song remains the same. These laws that have been violated against me are identical to the ones mentioned in the beginning of the last chapter. These same laws are extremely likely to be broken against you too, if they have not already.

Ignored Everything I Submitted

During a phone conference, Adler tried to steamroll hearing one of my motions. She only was ready and willing to address (and allow) Mihelic's motion to compel and was perfectly happy to skip right over my motion and would have done so if I had not immediately interrupted the calling of the next matter. During this hearing and as stated earlier, she did not respond to me when I firmly asked, "Are you reading anything I send you?" Instead, I was met with dead silence. Her failure to answer was undeniably a definitive answer.

During another hearing and after the lies in the court record and by Mihelic had been accepted as true—or just simply accepted—and after Mihelic stated that I filed a motion to dismiss, Adler said, "I see you've been busy writing another motion." The translation is: "I'm not going to read this one either, but it is just another nuisance that we have to tolerate."

Adler said in one of the first few telephonic hearings that I had "an elite level of knowledge of the law" and then insulted me by asking if I was an attorney, but she has proceeded to ignore everything I have said or submitted nonetheless. The statement is not true anyway. What I have is an elite level of knowledge of the *crime syndicate*. There is a big difference. I know how the world's largest crime syndicate truly operates and am the leading expert on the topic.

Conflicts of Interest

Mihelic and Judge Adler are both members of the following organizations. It is virtually impossible that they have never met at any respective social functions and do not have some sort of interpersonal relationship. This can certainly be viewed as a conflict of interest. The list is not intended to be exhaustive:

- Lawyers Club of San Diego

- San Diego Bankruptcy Forum

- National Conference of Bankruptcy Judges

- International Women's Insolvency and Restructuring Confederation

Not surprisingly, neither Adler nor Mihelic are members of the American Constitution Society or Christian Legal Society. It may not seem like a big deal, but, like a jigsaw puzzle, all pieces connected together reveal much more than a single piece by itself.

Regarding every phone conference associated with my bankruptcy in which I have ever participated, without exception, Adler asked someone else to write the court order whenever one needed to be created. In my case, it was always Mihelic whom she asked. She let the Department of Injustice be judge, jury, and executioner by having its personnel write the court's orders. It is bad enough having an opposing party write a court order since doing so is clearly a conflict of interest, but having a *government attorney who I proved has lied well in excess of thirty times (and repeatedly perjured herself) in just my single bankruptcy matter* do it is about as massive a conflict of interest imaginable anywhere on Earth.

In everything Mihelic has written—both her own papers and court orders—she has consistently omitted things that are true and added things that are false. Basically, a criminal created the court record and another one blessed it, and then the first criminal pointed to the court record that she created to support even more lies. Unsurprisingly, Mihelic effectively kept saying in all her papers, "Look at the court record." Of course that was what she was going to say. She basically wrote/engineered the (corrupt) court record.

I have said all along, "No! Look at the evidence instead," which nobody has done yet anywhere in the nation. It has become plainly apparent that there are two sets of rules: rules for people that the syndicate likes and rules for people that the syndicate doesn't like. If the information in this subsection doesn't blow your mind, then nothing will.

Words Omitted in Court Orders and Other Documents

Several documents and court orders had words omitted from them. The wording in one particular order was written with the phrase "and of any other communication from or to him" omitted in an attempt to conceal the clandestine contact from Michaud. The order says "[t]here is no evidence." There's plenty of evidence; it's just that some evidence is being hidden and/or ignored by the syndicate. This is just one example; there are many others.

Keep in mind that the words in the court orders are not Judge Adler's own words. They are really the words of Mihelic because Adler let Mihelic write the orders. But blame *cannot* be shifted away from Adler simply because Mihelic omitted key words and added lies in her papers and court orders that she truly authored. It is the judge's responsibility to either write her own orders or actually *look* at the evidence to verify whatever has been written in orders drafted by the Department of Injustice. Turning a blind eye to all of this is no excuse, especially when I repeatedly told Adler about the misconduct and criminal acts of Mihelic. In order to make things fit her narrative, Mihelic blatantly and wantonly ignored elements in the record and other documents and added untruths whenever it suited her to do so.....and Adler went along for the ride.

Blatant Bias

Judge Adler is heavily, Heavily, HEAVILY biased. She made overtly biased statements in telephonic hearings and explicitly in the court record.

One such statement was made in a tentative ruling, part of which is as follows: "Although it is premised, in part, on Defendant's [alleged] transfers of real property to avoid and frustrate creditors, it is not an action requesting recovery of a fraudulent transfer." Whenever anyone associated with a legal action does not use terms such as "alleged" when accusations are made but not yet proved in court, it not only flies in the face of conformance with due process, but it is constitutionally offensive—particularly when made by a so-called judge.

Another was made during a hearing. Adler asked Mihelic: "What will you need to be ready for trial?" She did not ask me the same question. Apparently, it was only important that Mihelic had whatever she deemed necessary to be ready for trial and win the case—not that justice was served. This is disturbing.

Judge Adler also granted every known oral motion from Mihelic but denied every single verbal motion and opposition from me—and there are many. All entries in the court record that state Mihelic's motions were "unopposed" are incorrect. The court took its time to allow me to file electronically. I did not oppose Mihelic in writing because I could not afford the added expense of printing and filing by U.S. mail, but I tried to state my positions verbally. Judge Adler prevented it. But she sure allowed Mihelic to present oral motions on several occasions. Finally, Mihelic asked for *at least* six or seven filing extensions, which is beyond outrageous—and even more outrageous for the syndicate to grant them all.

Lies Told

Judge Adler lied to me in one of the telephonic conferences when she said, "This isn't a criminal matter. You don't get a lawyer appointed to you," or something very similar.

She also lied in a related tentative ruling wherein she stated, "Sec. 1951(e)(1) [*sic*] is not relevant here as it relates only to prisoners." However, 28 U.S. Code § 1915(e)(1), says otherwise:

"The court may request an attorney to represent any person unable to afford counsel." This particular section does not apply just to prisoners. Moreover, the U.S. Supreme Court case *Maness v. Meyers* made clear that the appointing of counsel for low-income people in certain civil cases is not optional— but mandatory—and "that counsel must be appointed for any indigent witness, whether or not he is a party, in any proceeding in which his testimony can be compelled." Adler had already compelled my testimony.

In her same tentative ruling, she also lied about me not communicating with Mihelic. Yet again in this same ruling—one riddled with lies, and a falsified official record itself—Adler lied about the date I filed my Motion to Compel Disclosure and for Sanctions. She also lied in this ruling when she stated that I "altered evidence," which I did not do, but Mihelic certainly did do.

Basically, the Department of Injustice repeatedly falsely accused me and Judge Adler allowed it. So, what happened is that one of the criminals lied and the other swore by it. Judge Adler lied many other times, but those are not included in order to keep this chapter as brief as possible.

Unlikely Mathematical Odds

Perhaps the most striking evidence against Judge Adler is that she ruled at least twenty-two consecutive times against me whenever Mihelic opposed me. Odds of this purely happening by chance and *without bias or external influence* are 1 in 4,194,304, or less than 0.00002 percent. Incidentally, all told since the beginning of the civil case in Massachusetts mentioned at the start of this chapter, the syndicate has ruled against me fifty-one consecutive times whenever I have been opposed. Odds now become 1 in 2,251,799,813,685,248. The chance of hitting Powerball is 7,706,328 times greater since the odds of winning that particular lottery are *only* 1 in 292,201,338.

Conclusions of Law Based Solely on False Claims by Mihelic

Judge Adler repeatedly relied on false information from Mihelic to make rulings and issue orders. In effect, she made conclusions of law based on Mihelic's lies. One such instance concerns a ruling entered on April 29, 2021. This is just one example of many.

Predetermining the Outcome of the Case without Evidence

Similar to WWE, Judge Adler has played the role of Vince McMahon in predetermining the outcome of my case. She did this by ignoring facts and evidence and relied solely on lies from Mihelic to prevent my discharge and quite likely received a phone call from Michaud. I knew when the case began where it was going based upon the extreme level of fraud and corruption manifesting itself once again.

Mihelic's Misconduct and Criminal Acts Not Only Condoned.....but Me Chastised for Bringing Them to Light

The evidence I presented from the court record and elsewhere revealed Judge Adler's cavalier attitude towards misconduct and criminal acts—offenses that are perfectly fine if the offender is on the "right team." She simply didn't want to hear about any wrongdoing by government personnel, although she was quick to charge me falsely every chance she had. This alone is more than sufficient to sanction the judge, if not mandate suspension or immediate removal from the bench. Perhaps best illustrating Adler's detestable attitude towards me is my favorite quote by Doctor Ron Paul: "Truth is treason in the empire of lies."[1]

Violations of the Code of Conduct for United States Judges

Judge Adler's violations of the Code of Conduct for United States Judges are described in the subsections below.

Canon 2: A Judge Should Avoid Impropriety and the Appearance of Impropriety in All Activities

Section "A" of this canon of the code clearly states, "Respect for Law. A judge should respect and comply with the law and should act at all times in a manner that promotes public confidence in the integrity and impartiality of the judiciary." Because of Judge Adler's overt bias in my case and because she disregarded both federal statutory and case law and trampled the U.S. Constitution multiple times, she has obviously violated this canon.

Additionally, section "B" of this canon states, "Outside Influence. A judge should not allow family, social, political, financial, or other relationships to influence judicial conduct or judgment. A judge should neither lend the prestige of the judicial office to advance the private interests of the judge or others nor convey or permit others to convey the impression that they are in a special position to influence the judge."

Rest assured that *unredacted* phone records, if they could be obtained, would almost certainly reveal an outside influence. If Judge Adler communicated with Michaud, which she most likely did within the first couple weeks of my bankruptcy filing when he would have contacted her and asked her to block my bankruptcy as a favor to him, she is concealing it. I know a call was made and state this not only based on the evidence presented in the Violation of 28 U.S. Code § 1930 (f)(1) subsection above but also based on the evidence presented in the first Lies Told subsection above.

Canon 3: A Judge Should Perform the Duties of the Office Fairly, Impartially and Diligently

This canon of the code mandates that a "judge should perform those duties with respect for others, and should not engage in behavior that is harassing, abusive, prejudiced, or biased." From the preceding, it is quite clear this canon has been violated. Subsection (A)(1) of this canon goes further: "A judge should be faithful to, and maintain professional competence in, the law." Once again, from the preceding, there is no question that this canon has been violated—that Judge Adler has been *un*faithful to the law.

The wording of subsection (B)(6), "A judge should take appropriate action upon receipt of reliable information indicating the likelihood that a judge's conduct contravened this Code, that a judicial employee's conduct contravened the Code of Conduct for Judicial Employees, or that a lawyer violated applicable rules of professional conduct," dictates that judges should act whenever information is given about a lawyer who violated rules of professional conduct. During many phone conferences and in several court filings, I informed Adler that Mihelic repeatedly lied and committed perjury. I apprised Judge Adler of many other forms of misconduct. She gave no indication that she would take any action and instead completely ignored what I said.

Under subsection (1) of section (C), Disqualification, the canon reads as follows: "A judge shall disqualify himself or herself in a proceeding in which the judge's impartiality might reasonably be questioned, including but not limited to instances in which:" and continues under subsection (a) of this subsection: "the judge has a personal bias or prejudice concerning a party....." It is crystal clear that Judge Adler does not like me because, of course, I hate injustice, yet she made no effort to disqualify herself and furthermore wrongly denied my motion for recusal.

Adler is a horrible judge—representative of so many on the bench today who should be removed, if not imprisoned. If you doubt any of the information provided thus far in this chapter, visit the first link provided in it and see for yourself.

Abram Stuart Feuerstein

Sometimes maggots can be found feeding among the trash in the toxic waste dump. On such maggot is Feuerstein, an attorney for the Department of Injustice. During the earlier stages of my bankruptcy, he made at least one telephonic hearing appearance and filed papers in the matter on behalf of the federal government. He has either lied or supported the lies of Mihelic and also has no interest in justice but only cares about protecting his criminal friends. He is also the art collector mentioned in chapter five.

George Vincent Manahan

Manahan is the government attorney who is allegedly representing Mihelic, Adler, and Carroll in the civil lawsuit I was forced to bring against them. Despise knowing they have committed misconduct and crimes in the matter that precipitated it—the civil action they either started or were involved in during my bankruptcy—he is plowing ahead to fight me nonetheless. He has repeatedly tried to deflect blame from his criminal friends and place it on the U.S. government. He has also lied and contradicted himself in the motions and objections he has thus far filed.

Cameron Myles Gulden

Yet another government attorney who inhabits the toxic waste dump is Gulden. He is representing the syndicate in the appeal I have filed with the Bankruptcy Appellate Panel for the Ninth Circus. Like those before him, he is well aware of the misconduct and crimes that Mihelic, Adler, and Carroll committed and has seen the undeniable evidence I have against them yet refuses to do anything (corrective) about it. Instead of having a backbone and declining to represent them or reporting their heinous acts to his chain of command or internal oversight boards, he is also plowing ahead to fight me and perpetuate the fraud nevertheless.

Robert J. Faris

This particular piece of trash is a so-called federal judge in Hawaii. He does not like truth, law, or any light being shined on fraud, corruption, and other criminal activity within the syndicate, about which I freely write in all my court filings. He clearly proved that he is an enemy to free speech and due process and that he is hostile to the entire U.S. Constitution by ordering court staff to prevent me from filing papers in retaliation for my writings. He is one of two judges to do this—the other being a Massachusetts state judge. But to their credit and instead of trying to secretly hide their bias, they have essentially openly admitted it by blatantly trying to block my access to justice.....if there is such a thing anymore in today's courts here in Amerika.

Gary Allan Spraker

This lawyer in a black gown is a member of the federal court in Alaska. He is quite similar to Faris. He disregards facts and law and instead rules in favor of his friends. He thinks nothing is wrong with Mihelic and others at the Department of Injustice lying, breaking laws—at least eleven of them criminal—and violating the code of conduct, court rules of procedure, and the U.S. Constitution.

Julia Wagner Brand

Brand is a "judge" in the federal court system in California. And like the preceding two, she also disregards facts and law and instead rules in favor of her friends and likewise thinks that Mihelic and others in power should be able to break rules, commit crimes, and desecrate the Constitution with impunity. She and the two named above are some of the worst that infect the injustice system in the nation. They opted to put taxpayers on the hook for costs associated with wrongdoing by Adler, Mihelic, and the Department of Injustice.

Linda Lopez

Sometimes trash in the toxic waste dump may be hidden underneath other trash, and you have to dig to find it. Whatever staff attorney thus far ruled on my civil case in the U.S. District Court for the Southern District of California is the kind of trash hidden underneath trash named Judge Linda Lopez. She rubber-stamped whatever the staff attorney concocted in the process of protecting his or her criminal friends—Mihelic, Adler, and Carroll. Rather than actually take the time to look at the facts, evidence, pleadings, and whatnot and rule according to justice, Lopez decided to accept the garbage that the other piece of trash handed her and rule in opposition to justice.

THE BEGINNING OF THE CURRENT INFECTION

My experiences with the syndicate go back about three decades, but the bulk of my legal battles began nearly two decades ago when Alyssa L. Parent refused to pay me approximately $4,300 for consulting and HVAC services I rendered for her small business in 2002. In December of 2005, a lawyer supposedly working on my behalf, Mr. Alan Cohen, commenced a civil action in the corrupt Taunton District Court in the People's Republic of Massachusetts against Parent in order to collect the money.

Cohen, my first attorney of record, was frightened off the case because of false, unrelated statements made to him by Michaud, the attorney for Parent, which at the time was a violation of state criminal law 268 § 13B(1)(c)(v). Recall from the TRASH FOUND IN THE TOXIC WASTE DUMP section in this chapter that Michaud is the attorney who violated a multitude of rules and laws but was later appointed to the bench anyway and the aforementioned law magically changed soon afterward so that he could not be prosecuted for this particular felony.

I then obtained a second attorney, the late Leonard Eskenas. Despite my repeated attempts via various means to have him move the case forward, he did absolutely nothing and eventually had to be fired, reported to the oversight board, and sent a demand letter in order to force him to return my retainer in full. Miraculously, he had previously been given a public reprimand by the board for violation of the rules of professional conduct in an unrelated matter. Michaud intimidated Eskenas the same way he did Cohen by telling him the same lies.

Michaud made no effort whatsoever to file an answer or a counterclaim for nearly *nine years*, but instead chose to focus his time and effort on making completely mendacious statements to my attorneys in order to coerce them to withdraw from the case, and successfully managed to do so.

In August of 2014, upon a motion I filed for default judgment, the court rightfully awarded me a default judgment in the amount of $11,271.53 because the defendant, Parent, through her counsel, Michaud, had taken no *legal* action in the case, but instead had opted to take plenty of *illegal* action by obstructing justice through multiple violations of state law 268 § 13B(1)(c)(v).

Corruption began to rear its ugly head in September of 2014 when Michaud finally filed a fraudulent answer and counterclaim nearly *nine years* late as a result of the issuance of the default judgment against his client. I hired a third attorney to pursue the matter. Michaud intimidated this attorney just as he had done to my former attorneys. Despite working on the case for several months, this lawyer also withdrew.

The court illegally vacated on three different dates the original legitimate default judgment it had awarded me. The first time the court did so was as a favor to Michaud after it received a mere phone call from him—*before* he filed his motion to vacate and in flagrant violation of the rules of civil procedure. This was most likely done in an attempt to prevent the default judgment from taking full effect before any motion could be heard. I was first notified by email from the court in September of 2014 of the judgment being vacated.

Being fed up, I lodged a complaint against Michaud with the attorney oversight board, but because the attorney governing boards only discipline attorneys about 2 percent of the time out of all complaints received nationally, the complaint against him was summarily dismissed without investigation.[2] As a result, I filed a complaint against the oversight board with the state supreme judicial court for the board not doing its job. This was an exercise in futility. I filed other complaints against certain court personnel and other entities for various misconduct and crimes, the latter of which include perjury, fraud, conspiracy to commit fraud, misprision of felony, obstruction of justice, and falsifying evidence, records, and documents. These crimes are the same ones listed in the beginning of the last chapter. All these other complaints were equally futile and dismissed without investigation despite rock-solid evidence of wrongdoing.

In July of 2015, I filed a complaint with the judicial oversight board against Judge Kevan Cunningham for violating the rules of court, breaking criminal statutory law, acting under the "color of law", violating four judicial canons, and violating the U.S. Constitution. The complaint mentioned Cunningham's involvement as a co-conspirator in the mail fraud and racketeering case bought by federal prosecutors in U.S. district court in early 2014, but he somehow managed to avoid an indictment, a trial, and a subsequent conviction. My complaint against him was also summarily dismissed without investigation.

The following month, I filed a petition for interlocutory relief with the state supreme court in an effort to force the court to start following its own rules, laws, and the U.S. Constitution. This, of course, was also a complete waste of time since the petition was improperly dismissed.

After telling me not to contact the court, denying me a trial, holding clandestine hearings when the court knew I could not be present, and violating a myriad of rules of procedure and civil and criminal laws in a concerted effort to steer that case in the direction they wanted it to go, the syndicate awarded a $32,913.30 fraudulent judgment to Parent in November 2015. Coincidentally, this figure was quite close to the damages requested ($31,438.31) in my original MOTION FOR DEFAULT JUDGMENT.

The court, because of corruption, managed to convert a legitimate judgment in the amount of $11,271.53 given to me in August of 2014 into a fraudulent judgment for Parent in November of 2015 in the amount of $32,913.30. The syndicate did this despite my notification to the court prior to the trial date and by a third party on the trial date itself that the trial would need to be postponed due to my illness and me missing a flight. I received no notification from the court either in writing or verbally to the person who made the call that the trial would continue nonetheless.

The entire state court system in Massachusetts violated statutory law and rules of procedure that severely prejudiced my case. The court manipulated the record to cover its tracks regarding illegally vacating my original default judgment and violated rules of procedure because it was unhappy that I filed complaints with the governing boards, the Department of Injustice, and the Federal Bureau of Iniquity. Of course, I would not have to have done any of this if the court had followed rules and law in the first place. The court felt it could do whatever it wanted unchallenged. Specifically, it failed to notify me of judgments in the case, the status of my motion to vacate judgment, and almost everything else related to the case after withdrawal of my third attorney. Therefore, I was not apprised as to activity in the case, which is a violation of due process.

In December of 2015, upon immediately learning via other channels of the court's corrupt activity, I filed an APPEAL FROM JUDGMENT directly to the appellate division in an attempt to circumvent the systemic corruption in the Taunton court. However, this appeal was forwarded to the Taunton court despite my wishes. As I fully expected, the appellate division, the actual appeals court, and the state supreme court were no less corrupt than the Taunton District Court.

In the last paragraph of the APPEAL FROM JUDGMENT, I requested that any related hearing be set *after* June 1, 2016. However, the court nevertheless scheduled one in March 2016. I learned of this when speaking with the District Court Administrative Office in August of 2016 and inquiring how to file a complaint against the court. I also learned my APPEAL FROM JUDGMENT was denied at that hearing (big surprise) during the same conversation. The criminals at this division of the syndicate thus continued their course of corruption and clandestine activities unchallenged.

In August 2016, I filed a MOTION TO APPEAL LATE, but still well within the 180 days allowed by District/Municipal Courts Appellate Division Appeals Rule 14(b). The motion was filed at this time because I was not informed of the hearing held in March 2016 or of its results and was still awaiting the status of my APPEAL FROM JUDGMENT. Again, I was not expecting any activity prior to June of 2016 since I specifically requested any hearing be set after June 1, 2016. During the phone conversation of August 2016, I was incorrectly told the motion must be filed with the district court. State rules of civil procedure specifically contradict the information I was then given.

Possibly to give the illusion of following the rules to the external investigators with whom I filed complaints and after a long absence of notifications, the court finally notified me by U.S. mail of the hearing on the MOTION TO APPEAL LATE scheduled for September 2016.

Despite my appearance at the September 2016 hearing, my motion was denied, not surprisingly, by the corrupt court despite all the evidence I provided proving the crime, corruption, and violations of law. I filed several other appeals, petitions, and more with the syndicate in that state, but all of them were completely disregarded.

Unbeknownst to me, a new attorney for Parent entered the fraudulent judgment as a foreign judgment in Rhode Island in February of 2016 and attached property I have not owned since July 2014.

I learned of the judgment in early 2020 and filed a chapter 7 bankruptcy in February 2020 to prevent the imminent sale of the Rhode Island property and the loss of approximately 40 percent of my income as manager of the property. If I had been living in Rhode Island, I would have simply fought the matter there, had it dismissed, and not filed bankruptcy. However, I could not afford to be repeatedly travelling across the country to resolve the matter nor pay a local attorney to resolve it for me, which I would have had to have done since the relevant court would not allow a virtual hearing.

In July 2020, Mihelic filed a baseless complaint against me objecting to discharging the fraudulently incurred "debt" despite me telling her several times that the judgment was in fact fraudulent. The corrupt bankruptcy court entered a fraudulent order striking my answer and entering a default in June 2021 and a final order of judgment by default in August 2021. Various other fraudulent orders have been entered by the syndicate in California regarding this matter.

As a result of their crimes and misconduct, I have been forced to sue the responsible criminals—Mihelic, Adler, and Carroll—in state court. I specifically chose state court because the likelihood that they have friends there should be lower than in federal court. As of now, my bankruptcy and the associated case Mihelic filed are in the appellate court, and the lawsuit against the criminals is pending. So far, the courts here in California have proved to be only *slightly* less corrupt than those in Massachusetts.

Alarmingly, the tales of woe in this chapter and the last are not the exception; they are now the rule. While these two chapters form the crux of this book, seven and eight are nearly as important since they discuss not only corrective measures that can be taken but also how you can do your part.

Chapter 7: How to Clean and Disinfect the Toxic Waste Dump

Sometimes you just have to break open the disinfectant. Some jobs require it. — **Linda Evangelista**

Recent polls confirm that public confidence in legal institutions and lawyers is at historic lows. Gallup's June 2016 poll indicates that only 36 percent of Americans have a "great deal" or "quite a lot" of confidence in the Supreme Court, and only 23 percent feel that way about the criminal injustice system. How do lawyers fare? Only 15 percent of the public has a high degree of confidence in them. The questions are: where do we go from here, and how can public faith in lawyers be restored and a true legal system replace the current syndicate? The simple answer is that the fix is not going to be quick or easy, but below are twenty-one thought-provoking ways to effect a solution.

1. Get rid of immunity altogether, be it judicial, prosecutorial, or what have you. There is nothing at all in the U.S. Constitution about it. Immunity is something our wonderful syndicate members have bestowed upon themselves. They were kind enough to give themselves this privilege in a similar way that our legislators give themselves special health care plans and other perks. Take immunity out of the picture, and many, perhaps most, of our renegade judges would snap back into line for fear of being accountable to the public—as they really should be.

2. Separate the career paths for lawyers and judges and not allow any lawyers to be judges and vice versa. Training to become a lawyer would lead one to become a lawyer; training to become a judge would lead one to

become a judge. The two professions would have as much in common with each other as professional bowling and meteorology. This crossover from one profession to the other perpetuates the "good ol' boy" network. Take away the opportunity for favoritism, and favoritism should vanish.

3. If a person wants to be part of the injustice system, such as becoming a police officer, lawyer, clerk, or judge, spending some time in jail should be a prerequisite. The people responsible for sending others to prison should know what it is like. As responsibility and power increase, the length of incarceration should increase. A day in jail seems reasonable for a clerk. Maybe two days would suffice for a police officer, and possibly three to five days for judges at the highest court levels.

4. To discourage members of the injustice system from participating in corruption, penalties for them should automatically be more severe than for those outside of the system—something on the order of a factor of two or three. So, if a financial penalty for the average person is $10,000 for a particular criminal offense, it should be $20,000 or $30,000 for a judge or police officer, for example.

5. Get rid of arcane laws that are no longer applicable and laws that are completely idiotic. The sheer number of laws in this country is so overwhelmingly large,

lawmakers should have to get rid of a law if they want to create a new one. To accelerate the reduction, legislators would have to remove ten laws from the books for every new one they create, with the ratio dropping periodically until it reaches one-to-one in the next two or three decades perhaps.

6. Oversight organizations for lawyers and judges should have no more than one lawyer or judge on each. Every governing body would be mostly composed of educated lay people. The way it stands now, most of these boards consist primarily of lawyers and judges. Having the fox guard the henhouse is not the best way to keep the chickens safe.

7. Establish a truly independent, outside organization or committee of "moles" that acts as a check on the syndicate—almost like "secret shoppers" at retail stores. Each "mole" would observe courtroom proceedings unannounced and incognito and report corrupt judges, prosecutors, bailiffs, clerks, and others to the committee's superiors. This committee could even be part of the oversight organizations or at least be the appellate channel for them so that when the 98 percent of all complaints against lawyers and judges get swept under the rug as they do now, a citizen would have a real chance of redress. Information provided by this watchdog organization would be instrumental in supporting constitutional-friendly judges and keeping

horrendous judges away from the bench. "Moles" from such organization would visit courts randomly. They would be paid a low base salary but with different levels of commissions based upon what and how much corruption they uncovered, so they would be incentivized to find it and report it.

8. In a criminal case, if a defendant is found to be not guilty or the case is otherwise dismissed, the prosecutor and/or the alleged victim should pay the defendant's legal fees and other related costs. To deter malicious prosecutions, prosecutors would also pay some established percentage out of pocket to cover injuries to the defendant, such as wages lost during incarceration while awaiting trial. An independent panel would determine if a prosecution was mistaken or malicious. This would go a long way toward eliminating politics and establishing fair play in the criminal injustice system.

9. Make our prisons truly private with competition, not exclusively private so that a contract is given to only one corporation, possibly the lowest bidder. In our nation today, the majority of "privatized" prisons have it written into their contracts that the occupancy rate must be maintained at a relatively high level. This incentivizes the syndicate to fill prisons to capacity.

10. Law enforcement organizations across the country are issued various forms of weaponry that are highly dangerous. To

mitigate shooting innocent or unarmed people, training at all levels of law enforcement must be improved. At least some post-high school education should also be mandatory—two years of college, for instance.

11. Open records to the public for all complaints filed against syndicate members.

12. Establish term limits for all judges, prosecutors, and attorneys general who are appointed. The public would have the ability to extend their terms by voting or other mechanisms; however, unlike voting in political elections, even people who have served time would be allowed to vote. This is especially important if they have been victimized by the incumbent official. Any vengeful votes should be counteracted by votes of victims of the crimes.

13. Allow the public at any time to remove directly from office any judicial official either by petitioning, voting, or some other means. The removal would be automatic if a certain number of complaints are filed against the offender by different people, either within a certain time span or overall. Even if no change is made to the oversight organizations and all (or nearly all) complaints get rejected as they do today, the official would be removed nonetheless and only be reinstated by public action. To prevent baseless complaints from being filed, a minimal fee could be charged except

to those showing financial hardship. In places where officials are elected, the governor would appoint a temporary replacement, and new elections would be held within a certain time frame to elect a replacement for that position.

14. Remove the self-regulation of the legal profession and assign it to citizens' grand juries in each district that would not only hear complaints against lawyers, but would also hear complaints against judges.

15. Ensure that all judges have competition for their elected positions by making it easier for attorneys and other qualified people to accede, and actively find constitutional-friendly attorneys to successfully run against anti-constitutional incumbent judges.

16. Improve courtroom transparency and accessibility. Since courts are open to the public, there should be legislation and funds available to make sure that every courtroom has live streaming video that the public can readily access from the internet and later readily retrieve as well. Every courtroom would also be remotely monitored by people who have been victimized by the syndicate and by the "moles" described in provision seven above. Moreover, there would be a large software system in place that would ensure the courtroom audio/video was working at all times, and if not, let officials know they could *not* proceed with any

hearings until fixed. If they did, all rulings would be void.

17. Establish a national and state public official website and database to report the performance or conduct of a judge, an attorney, or another syndicate member, with a search capability and the ability to research different issues. Input to the database could be both positive and negative. This will highlight trends and areas that need improvement and inform members of the public about crucial information they now lack.

18. Restore the constitutional protection of a jury trial, which has been stripped away by many courts. Jury trials would be allowed for every adversarial legal matter. Requiring the losing party to pay jury fees would prevent any inundation of "work" for the courts since "slam dunk" cases would likely settle beforehand.

19. Use root cause analysis for judicial errors—a process for identifying the basic or causal factors that underlie variation in performance, including the occurrence or possible occurrence of a sentinel event. Sentinel events are judicial errors that lead to injury, an unexpected occurrence involving death, or serious physical or psychological injury.

20. Pressure elected officials to ask more important questions when they appoint judges to the bench anywhere in the nation.

They can still ask the standard hot button issues of the day, which will probably never go away—those being *Roe v. Wade*, gun control, and so on—but they *must* begin asking questions that probe deeper. The questions that are *far* more important to the commoner are:

- What are you going to do about big business and government winning the overwhelming majority of cases, with most being dismissed before ever making it to trial?[1] [2]

- What is your track record regarding dismissal rate of cases in favor of big business and government and against everyday people?

- How many judicial complaints have been filed against you and as an attorney prior, and what are the results of those that were not dismissed?

21. Require judges to take periodic polygraph tests.

There you have it. All are logical, straightforward ideas that would certainly have a positive impact, albeit many might be considered a pipedream. Nonetheless, implementing just half of them would tremendously improve our injustice system.

Provision twenty-one could be particularly effective and far-reaching. If there is a profession in this country that warrants taking a periodic polygraph exam—a lie detector test—it is the judicial profession. Every state and federal judge in the United States should be required to take a polygraph test, perhaps yearly, in order to safeguard the public from malfeasance within the syndicate. It should be a condition of employment for all judges.

Doing so would go a long way towards cleaning and disinfecting the toxic waste dump. The American Polygraph Association sets the standards for testing and maintains that polygraphs are "highly accurate" citing an accuracy rate above 90 percent. Polygraph tests are used by law enforcement during criminal investigations, to screen potential employees, and for probation officers to supervise sex offenders. And yet while government agencies use polygraph tests, it is mind-boggling that the syndicate won't allow them to be used as evidence.

Think about it; the syndicate routinely allows false information regarding documents to be admitted into evidence and allows people who have histories of lying and doing bad things, including felons convicted of heinous crimes, to testify in criminal proceedings at the request of prosecutors. But in the face of all those highly questionable sources of information, the syndicate disallows polygraph test results into evidence despite their high accuracy rate, which makes no sense. Polygraph test results can be challenged just like any other piece of evidence. But the syndicate is set up to restrict information that could be helpful in getting to the truth during legal proceedings despite test results having a relatively high accuracy rate and, in most cases, having a higher fidelity than what is currently being allowed into evidence.

There are a few states that are receptive to polygraph test results being used in court, but they are the exception and not the rule. In Florida, California, Georgia, and Nevada, polygraph test results can be used if the parties agree. In California lawyers can present the results to jurors and allow them to make up their minds. So, if polygraph tests are good enough for the courts in those states, it stands to reason that they should be good enough for all courts nationwide. Because fixing cases and accepting bribes is almost certainly a major problem with our judges, which Operation Greylord indicated that it is, common sense dictates the need for periodic polygraph testing of judges. Testing should be mandatory whenever a judge has been accused of judicial misconduct either via a complaint filed against him by a citizen or by another judge, the latter of which would likely be as rare as a planetary alignment.

Only three simple questions are needed:

1. Have you ever predetermined the outcome of a case contrary to evidence and facts?

2. Have you ever accepted a bribe of any kind?

3. Have you or others within your control been involved in misconduct, including, but not limited to, evidence tampering, falsifying official records, perjury, and fraud?

Sadly, in today's injustice system here in Amerika, this kind of test would likely weed out 50 percent or more of our judges. But as it stands, there are no truly effective ways to eliminate the bad apples. Furthermore, any judge who does not pass the test could be given the opportunity to take it again. Any judge disqualified by this method would lose any retirement benefits and be permanently removed from the bench. The threat of this kind of discipline hanging over their heads could be the catalyst to sterilize our injustice system. After thousands of judges are terminated in this way, their successors would be wary to have the same fate befall them.

It is a crime against the people when judges are allowed to operate in an unmonitored and unchecked system that allows them to line their pockets with money in court-related shenanigans. Unquestionably, the infestation of corrupt judges is a serious infection. Polygraph testing of judges can help provide the cure.

There are probably many other things that can be done to clean and disinfect the toxic waste dump. But we must start somewhere. Ideally, the best way to restore the system would be to take a wrecking ball to it and start from scratch because it is so diseased. However, it is not too late to do whatever we can to make *1984* fiction again.

Chapter 8: Don't Just Stand There; Do Something!

I swore never to be silent whenever and wherever human beings endure suffering and humiliation. We must always take sides. Neutrality helps the oppressor, never the victim. Silence encourages the tormentor, never the tormented. — **Elie Wiesel**

The United States, once the greatest nation, has had and continues to have its strengths and weaknesses. Regarding contemporary strengths as a nation, we have showed tremendous compassion towards other nations and the people within them. At one point not so long ago, we were the world's greatest creditor. We were the leaders in education, ingenuity, economic prosperity, opportunity, and so much more. This country gave birth to the constitutional republic. Prior to the glorious work of the Founding Fathers, countries had basically one of two main leadership options: monarchy or dictatorship. Pick your poison. While a monarchy is still both the best and worst form of organized government depending upon who is in power, there was no form of government in centuries past that could be considered consistently good over time. That all changed on September 17, 1787.

On that day when the Constitution was signed, little did anyone know that almost all countries of the world would later also have their own constitutions, many of which were modeled after ours, at least at one point. What the Framers did is nothing short of genius. Granted, the United States is not, never was, and never will be all baseball, hot dogs, and apple pie. Because it is filled with imperfect humans as is any other country, it had its strengths and weaknesses when it was created, and it still has them today.

Regarding contemporary weaknesses as a nation, the USA leads the world in many bad things. One, for example, is incarceration rate. Only China comes relatively close to incarcerating the total number of people that the United States does.[1]

However, on either a per capita or total-number basis, Amerika walks away with the blue ribbon. Ah yes, something of which to be proud.

As of fairly recently, the USA also leads the world in external debt.[2] In the short span of a few decades, it went from being the world's greatest creditor to its largest debtor. This in itself is amazing. Other areas where we crush the competition include postsecondary education costs per student, healthcare costs per person, and more shameful things.[3] [4] Keep in mind that these latter two first-place finishes might be excusable if we led the world in premier education and healthcare. We don't. As far as medicine goes, the United States barely cracks the world's top twenty best healthcare systems.[5] With regard to schooling, we ranked twenty-fourth and twenty-fifth in reading and science, respectively, as of 2015. In math we are barely on the radar screen.[6]

I address the aforementioned weaknesses during speaking engagements and particularly incarceration rate and other failures of the injustice system. With respect to repairing it, one of the analogies I make is that, in order for a table to stand, at least three legs are needed. So it is with restoring the *justice* system. Those three criteria are:

- education

- unification

- implementation

Without these key ingredients, we have no chance of (positive) change. Education is accomplished by reading both my currently published books and certain others, such as *You Have the Right to Remain Innocent* and *Motion for Justice: I Rest My Case*, and by referencing additional reliable resources.

Unification is accomplished by coming together as a nation. We've seen this happen several times in the past, for example: just prior to the Revolutionary War, after the attack of Pearl Harbor, and most recently after the 9/11 attacks. Unfortunately as of late, it usually takes something as drastic as the latter for us to unify. Without unifying, there can be no single, powerful, directed force. So many times have I seen grassroots organizations fail because they are too small, too unconnected, and too powerless.

Implementation is our weakest link. Americans have a lot of great qualities. We also have several weaknesses. Getting out of our comfort zones tops the list. Europe and Asia run circles around us in this department: whenever there is discontent in the hearts, there is unity in the streets. We are great at complaining on social media, but when the rubber should meet the road, not so much.

The injustice system is the institution that needs the most improvement. It is the one thing that is virtually guaranteed to negatively impact the average citizen sooner or later. If every person contributed just a small amount of time or money, the top problem plaguing the nation would no longer be a problem at all. A few simple things that anyone can do are as follows:

- Know what judges are good and bad in your state so you can remove the bad ones via voting where feasible.

- Keep an eye out for any of the things mentioned in chapter seven whereby you can provide input.

- Read and share this book and the ones mentioned on the previous page with as many people as possible.

With respect to voting for judges, this has a far greater impact at the local and personal level than voting for president of the United States. It is far more important in the grand scheme of things. Think about it. The president doesn't pass laws or do things that negatively impact *only* you, your business, or your loved ones. The next time you are in court, a malevolent judge who legislates from the bench and doesn't like you, your business, or loved ones certainly will have a negative impact.

Chapter 9: Why Should I care?

Why should I care? Why should I
care? — **Pete Townshend, "5:15"**

Perhaps one of our greatest weaknesses as a nation is our apathy towards things that do not immediately affect us. An appropriate quote by Martin Niemöller summarizes what happens when people do not care about something until it is too late[1]:

> First they came for the socialists, and I did not speak out—
> Because I was not a socialist.
>
> Then they came for the trade unionists, and I did not speak out—
> Because I was not a trade unionist.
>
> Then they came for the Jews, and I did not speak out—
> Because I was not a Jew.

Then they came for me—and there was no one left to speak for me.

We tend to care only when we or a loved one is directly and negatively impacted by something bad. But by then the damage is done. The biggest obstacle to overcome with regard to convincing people that the danger of our toxic waste dump is real has to do with preconceived notions they have. Overcoming these notions is a monumental task most of the time.

"Minds of Our Own," a fascinating three-part series about how people learn—or fail to learn, shows that people will maintain false information in their heads despite seeing evidence to the contrary.[2] This documentary was produced in 1997 by the Harvard-Smithsonian Center for Astrophysics. I highly recommend watching at least part two of this series and then rereading this book if you have any remaining doubts. In this particular part of the presentation, a junior high student who does remarkably well in his science class and seemingly understands the concept of photosynthesis fails to answer an interviewer's question correctly both before *and* after completion of the class. It boggles the mind, yet the evidence is there.

The first step in solving any problem is to recognize the fact that there is indeed a problem. This was true at the beginning of time. It is true today. And it will be true forever into the future. The biggest problem plaguing the nation *is* the injustice system. Why is it the biggest problem, you might ask? One reason is that other major problems only directly affect certain segments of the population.

Let us look at another problem that gets a lot of national attention, unemployment. This problem only directly affects people of a working age. The syndicate, on the other hand, can directly affect anyone with a pulse.....and even someone without a pulse—probate, for example, affects dead people, or their estates.

Let us look at yet another problem that also gets a lot of attention here in the West, obesity. No one can reasonably dispute that this is a major problem. Recent data show that more than 42 percent of the population in the USA is obese. This has increased from roughly 30 percent nearly two decades ago.[3] However, obesity and being overweight only directly affects people who are not fit. Remember, you can mostly choose to be fit or unfit. You can't always choose whether or not the syndicate will impact you.

These are just two examples, but if all the problems of this nation are put into one bucket and the toxic waste dump is put into another, the latter would outweigh the former in terms of cost to society—financial and otherwise—and total impact to people and their lives and liberties. The syndicate is a multi-trillion-dollar yearly industry that must be dismantled and rebuilt from the ground up.

If 100 random people were placed into a room, I guarantee that at least ninety of them would say they had already experienced the injustice system and that it was not anything pleasant. Things like being falsely accused, wrongly imprisoned, and whatnot do not typically arise during usual conversations. Family members, friends, and colleagues of yours would fit these same numbers, but you may not be aware of their sad sagas simply because the topic has not been discussed.

There are more than 50,000 innocent persons imprisoned in the "land of the free."[4] What makes you think you could not possibly be one of them? Do you think that doing nothing wrong and following the law precludes you from landing in prison? Do you think that being wrongly accused just does not happen or it is so rare that maybe only a handful of those incarcerated fall into that category? In answer to all of those questions, *nothing could be further from the truth!* You could be in prison right now.....or worse yet, already executed for a crime you did not commit. It is estimated that this has happened many times in the past.[5]

Temporarily put aside all the reasons for caring based upon self-preservation. Assume that you will hit the lottery: nailing a one-in-a-million shot of making it through life without ever being victimized by the syndicate. What about your children or grand children? Do you think they will also hit the metaphorical lottery? For all intents and purposes, chances are basically zero that your progeny will get through unscathed, with the chances constantly shrinking over time as the syndicate worsens.

It is the same with global warming, for instance. We take action today not to protect ourselves, but to protect our posterity. Contemporary action or inaction affects the planet—and our descendents—decades and centuries from now. If we are not proactive and do not take the corrective course of action to restore the *justice* system, we are deliberately condemning those yet to be born. We are burdening them with the worst problem this nation has ever known. We are being irresponsible citizens by not fighting for what is right, not just for ourselves, but for them.

Chapter 10: Final Thoughts

For the powerful, crimes are those that others commit. — **Noam Chomsky**

RAMPANT CORRUPTION

Nothing the syndicate does surprises me anymore. After reading this far, perhaps you can now say the same thing. The two examples given in chapters five and six highlight my sentiments, but remember that there are far more examples, many of which are even more outrageous. One additional example concerns a fairly recent notorious case.

That specific case was the criminal one underlying *Fields v. Wharrie* in which a judge not only accepted a bribe, but prosecutors fabricated evidence and coerced witnesses into providing false testimony in order to secure a conviction and a death sentence against Fields. None of my experiences even come close to rivaling the amount of corruption in that particular case. I wonder if there were any other undiscovered forms of corruption that would truly launch it into contention for the gold medal, if not winning it outright, among contemporary miscarriages of justice. Certainly, the witch trials of colonial America in the 1600s had more integrity.[1]

COMPETITION IS A GOOD THING

Any time something is truly private, there is competition, which is good for humanity. It keeps prices down and quality up. When competition is taken out of the picture, problems arise. This is why big business, big government, or big anything, for that matter, is bad. They—like the syndicate—all lack that crucial component.

GRASSROOTS ORGANIZATIONS

Sadly, there are a great number of people in my national network who have already fallen prey to the syndicate. This cannot be undone, but in the future, others can be protected from the same fate. Many grassroots organizations have formed in recent years. They have the problem correctly identified, but lack the correct solution. Most of them on social media do a lot of arm flailing and wheel spinning, but that is about all they produce other than complaints. For whatever reason, they don't have the resources, knowledge, tools, and wherewithal to attack and defeat the problem. The syndicate can be defeated, but the effort and force must be directed and delivered in one powerful, unified way.

THE INJUSTICE SYSTEM IS LIKE CANCER

One observation is that the injustice system is like cancer in two major ways. You can't just ignore cancer because you don't have it or think to yourself, "It won't affect me because I don't have it now, and I don't do anything risky that would cause me to get it," or think, "I know other people who have had it, but they smoked, and that was the cause." Like cancer, the injustice system can strike nearly anyone at any time and without that person doing anything wrong, immoral, or illegal.

The other way it mirrors the dreaded disease is that it has an extreme tendency to spread. One case can generate many others, and this is by design, of course. I am living proof of that. One case in which I was involved in the People's Republic of Massachusetts has now spawned *seven* other legal battles for me. And there may still be no light at the end of the tunnel. As described in chapter five, the original battle that Luis Sanchez fought has also been the genesis of additional lawsuits for him. Again, the system is designed to operate this way and generate "work" for itself.

GOOD COP, BAD COP

With respect to the large number of law enforcement officers in the nation mentioned in chapter one, a significant point can be made. Sometimes it is better to look at percentages; other times it is better to look at raw numbers as it is here. If you randomly select 100 people and find that only 1 percent of them are bad, the total is just one person. Even being ultra-conservative, let's assume only 1 percent of police are bad.

Don't get me wrong; good and bad exist in all professions. And as such, people can be impacted negatively by the bad performance of other people in those occupations. For example, a bad meteorologist might ruin your picnic, or a bad mechanic might destroy your car. A bad cop, however, can cost you your life. Now, back to that 1 percent. If 1 percent of police are bad, that means there are about 10,000 armed and dangerous additional criminals in society.

While I'm anti-police, I'm pro-policing. There's a big difference between the office and the act. Keep in mind the Founders had no concept of police, so there's no mention of a police force in the Constitution. We can do a far better job by means other than through government-employed officers— neighborhood watch groups, private security, and more. Moreover, when non-government individuals do bad things and commit crimes, it is *far* easier to hold them accountable. Successfully suing federal or government officials for wrongdoing and winning a settlement is becoming harder and harder.

GOOD LAWYER, BAD LAWYER

Personal experience has revealed that good lawyers and bad lawyers seem to gravitate towards different areas of practice. Regarding good ones, the overwhelming majority of them will normally be found in patent law, real estate law, and other "harmless" areas of law. Regarding bad ones, the overwhelming majority of them will usually be found in litigation, sometimes personal injury, and quite often as prosecutors.

CRIME

All crimes discussed in this book—such as perjury, fraud, obstruction of justice, and others—are only considered bad and prosecuted if the syndicate doesn't like you, that is, if you are not on the "right team." This fact is captured in this chapter's opening quote by Professor Chomsky. If the syndicate likes you, you have absolutely nothing to worry about. The translation is that if you're part of the syndicate, chances are that you're safe; if you're an ordinary citizen, you will get crucified if you break any laws.....and often even if you don't break any laws.

　　　　With regard to criminal matters, understand that the syndicate does *not* prosecute people because they break the law; they prosecute them because they piss off the wrong people. The "kids for cash" judges were targeted only for this very reason;

otherwise, they'd still be doing it today. It is almost a certainty that judges are doing similarly outrageous things now but are not being prosecuted because they are on the "right team."

Also, note that the United States has the highest overall number of crimes—by almost a factor of two—but it is barely in the top 75 for murder rate per capita.[2] [3] We come in a little less than halfway down the list at 74. Our murder or real crime rate is relatively low, but our overall crime rate is high. The data suggest that many "crimes" exist merely to keep members of the system busy and the prisons full.

PULLING THE WOOL OVER OUR EYES

An important point that was not covered elsewhere in the book concerns the big PR machine that has operated so well to brainwash Americans. We have all been fed a line of baloney that we have the best justice system (money can buy). The two most populous nations on Earth are putting us to shame and proving that fallacy. China is considering judicial reform according to chinadaily.com:

"A judge shall be held liable for illegal adjudication if he/she intentionally violates the laws in adjudication or commits any gross negligence resulting in any wrong judgment and causing any serious consequences; specifying the circumstances and conditions for exemption from responsibility for adjudication; on the principle that one who has powers shall assume corresponding responsibilities and one who is derelict in his duty shall be held liable, specifying the responsibility for supervision and management that a court president shall assume if he/she improperly exercises any power of supervision and management over trials due to intentional or gross negligence; and improving the procedures for the determination, investigation, review and affixation of responsibility in respect of misjudged cases to strictly hold judges liable for illegal adjudication."[4]

Of prime importance from the above is that judges should be liable for intentionally violating the law and gross negligence and that oversight needs to be improved. This is completely at odds with how our injustice system currently operates.

India has also taken the first step by acknowledging the corruption and the second by suggesting a plan as revealed in the *Times of India*: "'The government first needs to fill up these vacant posts. At the same time, those under suspicion need to be removed in order to instill public confidence,' P Prasanna Kumar, special public prosecutor CBI and NIA, told TOI. According to him, people's faith will be eroded if those under cloud continue to play the role of prosecutors."[5] Here in Amerika, officials in the syndicate have yet to take the *first* step.

VIDEO RECORDING IS CRUCIAL

One final thought concerns cameras worn by police officers, in their vehicles, and in the courtroom. What do you suspect would have happened in the murder of George Floyd, Eric Garner, or anyone else for that matter if there had been no video evidence? Your answer should be the same as what would have happened had there been no video evidence to at least partially vindicate Luis Sanchez whose ordeal was covered in chapter five. Perhaps the most important thing we can do *now* is to put in place recording devices everywhere we possibly can to hold public "servants" accountable. This is a relatively easy and inexpensive thing to do.

CONCLUSION

For those of you who have read this book and dismiss everything or nearly everything in it despite all the facts and evidence, I can almost guarantee that someday you or someone close to you will be struck with the disease otherwise known as the U.S. injustice system. You will then look back and reflect on the material covered in this book, perhaps even the quote by Niemöller in chapter nine, and think to yourself, "Yes, Tom was absolutely right." But by then the damage will likely already be done. I urge you to take action *now*.

For the rest of you, all is not lost. The future can be changed. Consider the remedial ideas discussed in chapters seven and eight—particularly reading *and* sharing the books mentioned with all the people whom you cherish. The sooner we act, the sooner we can fix the nation's top problem. An ounce of prevention is worth a pound of cure.

Cleaning the toxic waste dump will take a while. Things will not improve soon, but given enough time—and effort—improvement is possible. Also, the system won't change (positively) without putting all three legs on the table as discussed in the metaphor of chapter eight. Everybody will need to make a contribution—however small. Getting all this to happen is not by any means an impossible task. I firmly believe that together we can clean the toxic waste dump and accomplish great things. United we stand; divided we fall.

Appendix

One may well ask: "How can you advocate breaking some laws and obeying others?" The answer lies in the fact that there are two types of laws: just and unjust. I would be the first to advocate obeying just laws. One has not only a legal but a moral responsibility to obey just laws. Conversely, one has a moral responsibility to disobey unjust laws. I would agree with St. Augustine that "an unjust law is no law at all." — **Martin L. King, Jr**.

The Minutes of the Court are stated below:
Dated: March 19, 2018
11:07:01 AM

At the direction of:
/s/ KATIE BERNARDS-
GOODMAN
District Court Judge

by

/s/ MELODY SIVERTSON
District Court Clerk

3RD DIST. COURT - WEST JORDAN
SALT LAKE COUNTY, STATE OF UTAH

STATE OF UTAH,   : MINUTES
          Plaintiff,   : PRETRIAL CONFERENCE
                                         : NOTICE
                                         :
vs.   : Case No: 151400466 FS
LUIS FERNANDO SANCHEZ,   : Judge: KATIE BERNARDS-GOODMAN
          Defendant.   : Date: March 19, 2018

PRESENT
Clerk: melodys
Prosecutor: SWIFT, NATHANAEL L
The defendant is not in custody
Defendant failed to appear for this hearing
Defendant's Attorney(s): TORRENCE, DANIEL M

DEFENDANT INFORMATION
Date of birth: Defendant failed to appear for this hearing
Sheriff Office#: 294811
Audio
Tape Number: 32   Tape Count: 8.45/10.48

CHARGES
1. FAIL TO STOP AT COMMAND OF LAW ENFORCEME - 3rd Degree Felony
      Plea: Not Guilty
2. INTERFERENCE WITH ARRESTING OFFICER - Class B Misdemeanor
      Plea: Not Guilty
3. DRIVING UNDER THE INFLUENCE OF ALCOHOL/DRUGS - Class A Misdemeanor
      Plea: Not Guilty

HEARING

Defendant failed to appear. Court orders a warrant in the amount of $15,000 cash only.
Bond forfeiture proceedings to commence.

Printed: 03/19/18 11:07:00   Page 1 of 2

10:48
Case is called to advise defendant he is being taken in to custody on the outstanding
warrant.

PRETRIAL CONFERENCE
     Date: 03/22/2018
     Time: 09:00 a.m.
     Location: WJ Courtroom 32
               8080 SOUTH REDWOOD ROAD
               SUITE 1701
               WEST JORDAN, UT 84088
 Before Judge: KATIE BERNARDS-GOODMAN

Individuals needing special accommodations (including auxiliary communicative aids and
services) should call 3rd Dist. Court - West Jordan at (801)233-9700 three days prior
to the hearing. For TTY service call Utah Relay at 800-346-4128. The general
information phone number is (801) 233-9700.

WARRANT

Failed to appear for scheduled hearing
Cash only.
The defendant must appear.
Serve the warrant anytime.

UNITED STATES BANKRUPTCY COURT
SOUTHERN DISTRICT OF CALIFORNIA
Minute Order

Hearing Information:

ADV: 20-90093

UNITED STATES TRUSTEE VS THOMAS SCOTT

Debtor:	THOMAS SCOTT
Case Number:	20-01053-LA7	**Chapter:** 7
Date / Time / Room:	THURSDAY, JUNE 24, 2021 02:00 PM DEPARTMENT 2
Bankruptcy Judge:	LOUISE DeCARL ADLER
Courtroom Clerk:	KAREN EARCE
Reporter / ECR:	JENNIFER GIBSON

Matters:

1) MOTION FOR SANCTIONS FOR PURSUANT TO FED. R. BANKR. P. 7037(b)(2) AND 7037(d)(1) OR IN THE ALTERNATIVE, FOR A FINDING OF CONTEMPT OF COURT PURSUANT TO FED. R. BANKR. P. 7037(b)(1) FILED BY KRISTIN MIHELIC ON BEHALF OF UNITED STATES TRUSTEE

2) U.S. TRUSTEE'S MOTION TO EXTEND DISCOVERY DEADLINES FILED BY KRISTIN MIHELIC ON BEHALF OF UNITED STATES TRUSTEE (from 4/29/21)

3) PRE-TRIAL STATUS CONFERENCE (from 4/29/21)

Appearances:

KRISTIN MIHELIC, ATTORNEY FOR UNITED STATES TRUSTEE (Tele)
THOMAS SCOTT (Tele)

Disposition:

1) Tentative Ruling of the Court is affirmed, except for the portion regarding the U.S. Trustee's additional request for monetary sanctions, that portion is withdrawn by Ms. Mihelic & vacated by the Court.
The order is to be lodged by Ms. Mihelic.

2-3) Tentative Ruling of the Court is affirmed.

132

References

Chapter 1

[1] https://www.merriam-webster.com/dictionary/syndicate
[2] https://usafacts.org/articles/police-departments-explained/
[3] https://www.statista.com/statistics/1087407/number-judges-magistrates-judicial-workers-united-states/
[4] https://www.zippia.com/prosecutor-jobs/demographics/
[5] https://www.worldatlas.com/articles/list-of-countries-by-number-of-police-officers.html
[6] https://www.economist.com/china/2015/09/24/judging-judges
[7] https://www.statista.com/statistics/1170564/india-number-of-judges/
[8] .https://www.uscourts.gov/sites/default/files/fy_2021_congressional_budget_summary_0.pdf
[9] https://www.americanactionforum.org/research/the-economic-costs-of-the-u-s-criminal-justice-system/
[10] .https://en.wikipedia.org/wiki/List_of_countries_by_government_budget
[11] https://www.statista.com/statistics/1049749/china-public-security-spending-by-government-level/
[12] https://www.washingtonpost.com/politics/2019/06/24/do-mexican-drug-cartels-make-billion-year/
[13] https://www.theguardian.com/world/2014/mar/26/ndrangheta-mafia-mcdonalds-deutsche-bank-study
[14] https://www.reuters.com/article/italy-mafia-idUSL6N0ALDMN20130116
[15] https://www.bbc.com/news/world-europe-42794848
[16] https://www.washingtontimes.com/news/2009/mar/03/100000-foot-soldiers-in-cartels/
[17] https://deathpenalty.procon.org/us-executions/
[18] Justice Deferred - Slate. http://www.slate.com/articles/news_and_politics/jurisprudence/2015/03/cameron_todd_willingham_prosecutor_john_jackson_charges_corrupt_prosecution.html.
[19] https://nypost.com/2014/02/23/film-details-teens-struggles-in-state-detention-in-payoff-scandal/

Chapter 2

[1] Richard Langworth, *Churchill by Himself: The Definitive Collection of Quotations* (United Kingdom: Ebury Press, 2008), p. 574; also stated in the House of Commons, November 11, 1947
[2] https://founders.archives.gov/documents/Jefferson/98-01-02-1540

Chapter 3

[1] Sara Naheedy, Tom Scott, Stack the Legal Odds in Your Favor (United States: Smart Play Publishing, 2016), p. 29.

[2] https://www.uscourts.gov/statistics-reports/complaints-against-judges-judicial-business-2015

[3] https://www.ncsc.org/__data/assets/pdf_file/0026/18881/study-of-state-judicial-discipline-sanctions.pdf

[4] https://www.motherjones.com/politics/2016/03/time-merrick-garland-was-accused-protecting-fellow-judge-charged-ethics-violations/

Chapter 4

[1] Fred R. Shapiro, The University of Chicago Law Review, Volume 88.7 (November 2021), p. 1602

[2] .https://www.abajournal.com/news/article/posner_most_judges_regard_pro_se_litigants_as_kind_of_trash_nor_worth_the_t

[3] .https://www.abajournal.com/news/article/posner_most_judges_regard_pro_se_litigants_as_kind_of_trash_nor_worth_the_t

[4] Former Appellate Judge Richard Posner, https://promarket.org/2017/03/28/richard-posner-real-corruption-ownership-congress-rich/, March 28, 2017.

[5] Adam Liptak, https://www.nytimes.com/2017/09/11/us/politics/judge-richard-posner-retirement.html, September 11, 2017.

[6] Jeffrey M. Jones, https://news.gallup.com/poll/354908/approval-supreme-court-down-new-low.aspx, September 23, 2021.

[7] Kevin Bliss, https://www.prisonlegalnews.org/news/2020/jan/9/former-seventh-circuit-judge-posner-founds-short-lived-project-help-pro-se-litigants/, January 9, 2020.

Chapter 5

[1] Pete Townshend, The Who, It's Hard, "Eminence Front" (United Kingdom: Polydor Records Ltd., 1982).

[2] https://www.fox13now.com/news/crime/unified-police-officer-charged-with-being-high-on-fentanyl-while-on-duty

[3] https://casetext.com/case/robinson-v-bernards-goodman

[4] https://www.sltrib.com/news/2020/10/31/utah-man-sues-public/

[5] https://law.justia.com/cases/utah/court-of-appeals-published/2020/20190250-ca.html

[6] https://mydefenseguide.org/massive-court-corruption/

Chapter 6

[1] Dr. Ron Paul, *The Revolution: A Manifesto* (United States: Grand Central Publishing, 2008), preface, p. 5.

[2] Sara Naheedy, Tom Scott, *Stack the Legal Odds in Your Favor* (United States: Smart Play Publishing, 2016), p. 16.

Chapter 7

[1] https://www.theatlantic.com/ideas/archive/2018/07/big-business-keeps-winning-at-the-supreme-court/564260/

[2].https://www.washingtonpost.com/news/posteverything/wp/2017/06/26/why-big-business-keeps-winning-at-the-supreme-court/

Chapter 8

[1] https://en.wikipedia.org/wiki/List_of_countries_by_incarceration_rate

[2] https://en.wikipedia.org/wiki/List_of_countries_by_external_debt

[3] https://www.investopedia.com/ask/answers/020915/what-country-spends-most-education.asp

[4] https://worldpopulationreview.com/country-rankings/health-care-costs-by-country

[5] https://worldpopulationreview.com/country-rankings/best-healthcare-in-the-world

[6] https://www.mathnasium.com/Pisaworldwiderank

Chapter 9

[1] https://en.wikipedia.org/wiki/First_they_came_...

[2] https://www.learner.org/series/minds-of-our-own/

[3] https://www.cdc.gov/obesity/data/adult.html

[4] Sara Naheedy, Tom Scott, *Stack the Legal Odds in Your Favor* (United States: Smart Play Publishing, 2016), p. 7.

[5] Justice Deferred - Slate.
http://www.slate.com/articles/news_and_politics/jurisprudence/2015/03/cameron_todd_willingham_prosecutor_john_jackson_charges_corrupt_prosecution.html.

Chapter 10

[1] Sara Naheedy, Tom Scott, *Stack the Legal Odds in Your Favor* (United States: Smart Play Publishing, 2016), p. 31-32.

[2] https://www.nationmaster.com/country-info/stats/Crime/Total-crimes
[3].https://en.wikipedia.org/wiki/List_of_countries_by_intentional_homicide_rate
[4] http://www.chinadaily.com.cn/china/2017-02/27/content_28361584_6.htm
[5] https://timesofindia.indiatimes.com/city/bengaluru/just-480-public-prosecutors-to-handle-6-3l-criminal-cases/articleshow/67616075.cms

Most of us.....thought that justice came into being automatically, that virtue was its own reward, that good would triumph over evil. But.....we know this just isn't true. Individual human beings have to create justice. And this is not easy because the truth often poses a threat to power. And one often has to fight power at great risk to themselves. The truth is the most important value we have, because if the truth does not endure, if the government murders truth, if we cannot respect the hearts of these people, then this is not the country in which I was born, and it's certainly not the country I want to die in. — **Kevin Costner, *JFK***

CPSIA information can be obtained
at www.ICGtesting.com
Printed in the USA
LVHW050550301222
736155LV00004B/542

9 780996 592970